SURE YOU WILL TRULY BE A
GREAT MISSION & SERVANT
OF THE LORD

COVENANT VERSES

THE BOOK OF MORMON

Millennial Mind Publishing
An imprint of American Book Publishing
American Book Publishing
P.O. Box 65624
Salt Lake City, UT 84165
www.american-book.com
Printed in the United States of America on acid-free paper.

Covenant Verses: The Book of Mormon

Designed by Brian MacMullin, design@american-book.com

Publisher's Note: *This publication is designed to provide accurate and authoritative information in regard to the subject matter covered. It is sold or distributed with the understanding that the publisher and author is not engaged in rendering legal, accounting, or other professional service. If legal advice or other expert assistance is required, the services of a competent professional person in a consultation capacity should be sought.*

ISBN 1-58982-160-2

Floyd W. Gowans, Floyd W., Covenant Verses: The Book of Mormon

---

Special Sales

COVENANT VERSES
THE BOOK OF MORMON

FLOYD W. GOWANS

Foreword by L. Edward Brown

Dedication

I dedicate this book to the men, women, and youth of the world who have not yet learned to feast upon the Scriptures. I send this work to you with the hope that it will motivate you to experience the daily spiritual feast that comes when you are submerged in the Word of God.

Foreword

The Book of Mormon stands as a colossus among books of Scripture. It testifies boldly of God's concern for and interaction with mankind. In fact, it declares that "man is that he might have joy" (2 Nephi 2:25). It offers great promises to all who ponder its teachings, indicating that as one studies prayerfully the doctrines found therein, and applies them unto oneself, that person has hope (1 Nephi 19:23–24).

The two major purposes for the coming forth of *The Book of Mormon* in our day are expressed on its title page. First, and foremost, this incomparable book of Scripture resoundingly and unequivocally testifies that "…JESUS is the CHRIST, the ETERNAL GOD, manifesting himself unto all nations." Second, this book of Scripture, which has come forth in the "…times of the restitution of all things," spoken of by Peter in Acts 3:21, shows:

> ...unto the remnant of the House of Israel what great things the Lord hath done for their fathers; and that they may know the covenants of the Lord, that they are not cast off forever. (Underlining mine)

The Book of Mormon offers reassurance and hope to those who qualify as members in the House of Israel, God's covenant people. However, it explains, as does Paul, that membership in the House of Israel is not based solely on genetics or geography. Paul taught the following to the Galatians:

> For ye are all the children of God by faith in Christ Jesus. For as many of you as have been baptized into Christ have put on Christ. There is neither Jew nor Greek, there is neither bond nor free, there is neither male nor female: for ye are all one in Christ Jesus. And if ye be Christ's, then are ye Abraham's seed, and heirs according to the promise. (Galatians 3:26–29)

I repeat for emphasis, "...then are ye Abraham's seed, and heirs according to the promise." Entrance into the House of Israel and access to the promises, or covenants, made by the God of Abraham, Isaac, and Jacob are offered to all.

The Book of Mormon stands as a monumental witness to this truth. Its pages are replete with promises that all may join the House of Israel, and that, having done so, they become full-fledged heirs to all of the promises God has extended through the fathers. At His appearance in the land called bountiful, as recorded in 3 Nephi 21:22, the resurrected Lord declares:

But if they will repent and hearken unto my words, and harden not their hearts, I will establish my church among them, and they shall come in unto the covenant and be numbered among this the remnant of Jacob...

The Book of Mormon is a book full of promises for all who will repent, be baptized, and become heirs according to the covenant found in Romans 8:16–17:

The Spirit itself beareth witness with our spirit, that we are the children of God:

And if children, then heirs; heirs of God, and joint-heirs with Christ; if so be that we suffer with him, that we may be also glorified together.

Brother Floyd W. Gowans has taken upon himself the gigantic task of identifying covenants with the associated promises thus available to us. Using an "if-then" formula, he lists the covenants that God made with His people and the obedience required of each individual to receive the promises made through those covenants. What a blessing this work will be to those who dissect its contents and reflect upon the written word.

Brother Gowans offers the reader a unique look into *The Book of Mormon.* One impression which will not escape the conscientious reader will be the certainty that the Master intends to extend to all who will come to Him everything He has. This is so beautifully illustrated in a covenant verse cited on page 211 by brother Gowans:

> Behold, I am he who was prepared from the foundation of the world to redeem my people. Behold, I am Jesus Christ. I am the Father and the Son. In me shall all mankind have life, and that eternally, even they who shall believe on my name; and they shall become my sons and my daughters. (Ether 3:14)

As one reads Brother Gowans's wonderful book, one will indeed have hope for the future and know that the Lord has not forgotten His covenant people, and that He is vitally involved in the affairs of humankind.

L. Edward Brown

Preface

In 1996, as a part of my daily Scripture study and as a result of my calling as Stake Mission President in the Omaha, Nebraska, Papillion Stake, I discovered what I have come to call "covenant verses." This discovery was so fascinating that I began to search for all the covenant verses I could find. As I found them, I marked them, became keenly aware of the hundreds of promises that the Scriptures contain, and felt inspired to seek after those promises.

I think that one of the reasons these covenant verses were so fascinating is that as many times as I had read the Scriptures, I had never given them due notice. I read past them, not appreciating what I was reading, or what the Lord was offering me.

As I studied these covenant verses, I noticed that I was personalizing them by rewording them into everyday language. I decided that I would rewrite them in my own words. I also discovered that if I wrote them in an "if" and "then" format, they became much easier to remember. It helped me better realize what I needed to do to obtain the promised blessings. I accumulated over fifteen hundred covenant verses after scrutinizing the texts.

I began to wonder if this work would be something in which others would be interested, so I continued to refine it. As it came to a point where I thought it might be presentable to someone else, I gave it to my mother and father. I asked them to look at it as if it were a book that they had simply found on a shelf at the bookstore. Would it interest them? Both my mother and father were very impressed. They showed it to a friend, who was likewise impressed. However, they all thought it was too lengthy; it was over 550 pages.

Next, I decided that it was time to take it to my former mission president, Brother L. Edward Brown, who had expressed an interest in it. He was also very impressed. He stated that as a former instructor in the Church Education System, he liked how it was in a chronological format, realizing how helpful that format would be in searching the Scriptures, and in teaching the promises they contain. I told him of the concern my parents and their friend had because of its size. He suggested that I break it down into the individual books of Scripture and publish it in four volumes. He further suggested that I prepare *The Book of Mormon* section for publication and have it available for 2004, when The Church of Jesus Christ of Latter-day Saints studies *The Book of Mormon*. Then, I could prepare the other sections over the next three years: the *Doctrine and Covenants* and *Pearl of Great Price*, *The Old Testament*, and finally *The New Testament*. This was the right idea. Therefore, I began preparing the *Book of Mormon* section.

If this book is studied along with *The Book of Mormon*, you will find it uplifting, and it will inspire you to make a daily habit of feasting upon the Scriptures. It will help you learn to personalize the Scriptures and "liken the scriptures unto yourself" (1 Nephi 19:24). A desire to obtain the blessings will grow within you. You will learn what sacrifices you need to make in order to obtain those blessings. The Spirit of God will be with you if you invite Him to assist you in your daily, diligent study of the Scriptures. I know this from my own, personal experience.

Introduction

2 Nephi 32:3 calls us to "feast upon the words of Christ…." This is truly a commandment to all, for a diligent, daily study of the Scriptures is a spiritual feast.

Since I started to feast upon the Scriptures, I discovered that the desire cannot be satiated. The more I feast, the more I am fed by the Spirit of God. But unlike regular eating, in which my body is filled, and in which the desire to eat diminishes, the desire to feed on the words of Christ only begets more desire.

What is the difference between feasting upon the Scriptures and simply reading them? To me, a feast is a joyful experience and a celebration with great meaning. I believe that our study of the Scriptures should also be a joyful experience. In order to have a feast experience rather than one of routine, one must study with a goal and purpose in mind. Each time I embark on a new reading and study, I prayerfully select a new gospel topic to research.

Several years ago I noticed, as I was studying the Scriptures, that many of the teachings of Christ and His prophets were taught in covenant form. These covenants were given in easy-to-follow steps. Following these steps will result in our obtaining wonderful blessings. I call these steps "covenant verses." One very simple, familiar covenant verse is found in 3 Nephi 13:33, "But seek ye first the kingdom of God and his righteousness, and all these things shall be added unto you." The Lord says that if I seek His kingdom first, then all things shall be added to me. The Scriptures are full of these beautiful covenant verses that promise us blessings should we read, feast, and apply them in our lives.

Not only do verses speak of blessings, but they also warn us. These warning verses are patterned after the covenant verses. For example, in 3 Nephi 12:20, the Savior states, "…except ye shall keep my commandments, which I have commanded you at this time, ye shall in no case enter into the kingdom of heaven." The Lord says that if I do not keep His commandments, then I cannot enter into the kingdom of heaven. Just as the covenant verses are a sign of the Lord's love for us, these warnings are a sign of His mercy.

Most of us already understand the nature of a covenant. In most cases, a covenant is an agreement between two individuals, where the first individual agrees to perform a certain function for the second individual, and the second individual agrees to compensate the first when the function is complete to his or her satisfaction. Covenants are made between God and man for very specific purposes. Covenants offer us opportunities to learn, to grow spiritually, to protect us from evil, to maintain our freedoms and liberties, to keep us on the strait (restricted) and narrow path, and ultimately to bring us back into the presence of God. For example, in Mosiah 24:13 we see how God will deliver His people out of bondage because of the covenant they have made with Him: "…I know of the covenant which ye have made unto me; and I will covenant with my people and deliver them out of bondage."

As we come to know Jesus Christ, learn to believe Him, and desire these promised blessings, He invites us to follow Him. We do so by obeying what He teaches us. Many of these simple covenant verses are found in His teachings.

Our Savior follows a very simple and basic pattern in His covenants: "If you do an action I command, then I will bless you with what I have promised." We see in the Scriptures how He invites both individuals and nations to make and keep covenants. In 1 Nephi 11:6, it is written, "…And blessed art thou, Nephi, because thou believest in the Son of the most high God; wherefore, thou shalt behold the things which thou hast desired." Then, in 1 Nephi 4:14, "Inasmuch as thy seed shall keep my commandments, they shall prosper in the land of promise."

It is my desire to search out the covenant verses that God invites us to enter into with Him recorded in Scripture. I fear that many of us fail to see and recognize the amazing opportunities for blessings if we are simply reading the Scriptures and not learning to study and feast. It is vital that we stop, recognize, and follow the steps outlined in the covenants. Of course, most of these are not so simple that they can be accomplished in a minute or two, or even in a day, but are processes that may take a lifetime.

In Mormon 8:18, we learn that God is not a partial God: "For I know that God is not a partial God, neither a changeable being; but he is unchangeable from all eternity to all eternity." Knowing this, we can be assured that God desires that we obtain all the blessings that He has for His children. We can have absolute faith that He will fulfill His part of the covenants. He will bless us the same as He has blessed others, if we will pay the price required for those blessings. In other words, if we will follow the steps that He has outlined as necessary for us to accomplish, we will receive the promised blessings. We must remember, too, that it will be in the Lord's timeline that those blessings come, not in ours.

In the example mentioned above, 3 Nephi 13:33, what is the covenant? What does the Lord expect of us and what is the promised blessing that will come if we do what is expected? To help us understand and comprehend these verses, and to make them more meaningful, I try to personalize them. I have tried to reword most of these covenant verses to an "if-then," cause-and-effect relationship, and at the same time personalize them to myself by using everyday language and grammar. I personalized 3 Nephi 13:33 this way: "If I put the kingdom of God first in my life, then He will give me all His promised blessings." Instead of a generality, and by using a cause-effect relationship, the verse has become simple to follow as a covenant.

Sometimes, there are covenant verses that do not seem to apply to me. Rather than leaving them out, I try to find the principle being taught and apply the principle to myself. For example, in 2 Nephi 10:14, the Nephites are told, "He that raiseth up a king against me shall perish, for I, the Lord, the king of heaven, will be their king, and I will be a light unto them forever, that hear my words." Even though this covenant verse is speaking directly to the Nephites, we can still apply the principle to ourselves. The principle is: The Lord is our King; nothing should ever come between us and God. I can make it personal by rewording the Scripture to say, "If I lift up myself in pride, thinking that I do not need the Lord, or if I exercise unrighteous dominion in my home, then I will perish." Am I not in essence raising myself up as a king against or in place of the Lord?

The Scriptures teach us in a very plain and clear way the covenants into which we must enter in order to be saved in the kingdom of God. I call these, for this book's sake, "eternal" covenants. An example of this is found in 3 Nephi 11:33, "And whoso believeth in me, and is baptized, the same shall be saved; and they are they who shall inherit the kingdom of God." How would you personalize this Scripture to yourself? This is how I did it: "If I believe in Jesus Christ, and am baptized, then I will be saved and inherit the kingdom of God."

Covenant verses throughout the Scriptures teach us what we can do from day to day to help us keep the "eternal" covenants, and ultimately be saved. An example of this is 1 Nephi 19:24, "Wherefore I spake unto them, saying: Hear ye the words of the prophet…and liken them unto yourselves, that ye may have hope…." I personalized this verse this way: "If I hear the words of Isaiah and liken them unto myself, then I will have hope." Baptism is a one-time, "eternal" covenant. What we *do* from day to day helps us keep our baptismal covenants. Hearkening unto the prophets and learning to liken the Scriptures to myself will give me hope, which will help me keep my baptismal covenants.

It is important that we learn to apply the Scriptures to ourselves, apply the principles that the Scriptures teach us, and use them daily. As you study the Scriptures, I hope you will discover a new purpose for reading and studying them. For example, will you find answers and solutions to problems? Will you find avenues to greater spiritual growth? Will you find help in sharing the gospel as a missionary or as a parent or as a friend? Will you learn more about the covenants made and how you can better keep them? Will you find ways in which you can grow in spiritual strength and testimony? Will you find access to special, needed blessings?

In the text of this book, I have first quoted a verse, or several verses, that contain a covenant. Then my own personal interpretation is written below the quotation of Scripture. This is how I have "likened the scriptures unto myself" (1 Nephi 19:24). You may very well "liken them" differently for yourself. I have been very prayerful in trying to ensure that each verse is meaningful and helpful, as I try to find a way to use each one personally. *These explanations are not in any way meant to establish or interpret the doctrine of The Church of Jesus Christ of Latter-day Saints.* They are my own prayerful considerations that I share in hope that they may be of help to you.

At the end of the book there is an appendix. Here you will find many very meaningful questions that we often ask ourselves or that others ask us. Associated with those questions will be the page numbers of the scriptural answers. Here is an example: *What must I do for the Lord to visit me?* The answers are found on pages 26, 29, 32, 33, 46, 53, 54, 176, 177, 211.

In this particular volume, I have extracted verses only from *The Book of Mormon, Another Testament of Jesus Christ*. I hope to follow this volume with additional volumes, one from the *Doctrine and Covenants* and *Pearl of Great Price*, one from the *Old Testament*, and the final one from the *New Testament*.

Contents

1 Nephi

1:4 For it came to pass in the commencement of the first year of the reign of Zedekiah, king of Judah, (my father, Lehi, having dwelt at Jerusalem in all his days); and in that same year there came many prophets, prophesying unto the people that they must repent, or the great city Jerusalem must be destroyed.

If I repent, then I will not be destroyed spiritually.

1:12 And it came to pass that as he read, he was filled with the Spirit of the Lord.

If I read (and study) the Scriptures, then I will be filled with the Spirit.

1:14 And it came to pass that when my father had read and seen many great and marvelous things, he did exclaim many things unto the Lord; such as: Great and marvelous are thy works, O Lord God Almighty! Thy throne is high in the heavens, and thy power, and goodness, and mercy are over all the inhabitants of the earth; and, because thou art merciful, thou wilt not suffer those who come unto thee that they shall perish!

If I come unto the Lord, then I will not perish.

2:16 And it came to pass that I, Nephi, being exceedingly young, nevertheless being large in stature, and also having great desires to know of the mysteries of God, wherefore, I did cry unto the Lord; and behold he did visit me, and did soften my heart that I did believe all the words which had been spoken by my father; wherefore, I did not rebel against him like unto my brothers.

If I desire to know the mysteries of God, and I pray to Him to know them, then He will visit me, and will soften my heart that I will believe the testimonies born to me by my father, mother, church leaders, and others.

2:20 And inasmuch as ye shall keep my commandments, ye shall prosper, and shall be led to a land of promise; yea, even a land which I have prepared for you; yea, a land which is choice above all other lands.

If I keep the commandments, then I will prosper, and I will be led to and inherit the celestial kingdom, which is choice above all.

2:21 And inasmuch as thy brethren shall rebel against thee, they shall be cut off from the presence of the Lord.

If I rebel, then I will be cut off from the presence of the Lord.

> **3:6** Therefore go, my son, and thou shalt be favored of the Lord, because thou hast not murmured.

If I do not murmur against the Lord or His servants, then the Lord will favor me.

> **3:7** And it came to pass that I, Nephi, said unto my father: I will go and do the things which the Lord hath commanded, for I know that the Lord giveth no commandments unto the children of men, save he shall prepare a way for them that they may accomplish the thing which he commandeth them.

If I exercise faith in the Lord, knowing that He will prepare a way for me to accomplish His will, then He will not let me fail.

> **3:18** For behold, they have rejected the words of the prophets. Wherefore, if my father should dwell in the land after he hath been commanded to flee out of the land, behold, he would also perish. Wherefore, it must needs be that he flee out of the land.

If I do the will of the Lord, then I will not perish spiritually.

> **4:14** And now, when I, Nephi, had heard these words, I remembered the words of the Lord which he spake unto me in the wilderness, saying that: Inasmuch as thy seed shall keep my commandments, they shall prosper in the land of promise.

If I study the Scriptures and ponder them, and if I continue to be prayerful, then the Holy Ghost will bring back to my remembrance the promises made to me, and I will be able to keep focused on the most important things in my life. (See 1 Nephi 2:20 above.)

6:4 For the fulness of mine intent is that I may persuade men to come unto the God of Abraham, and the God of Isaac, and the God of Jacob, and be saved.

If I come to God, then I will be saved.

7:12 Yea, and how is it that ye have forgotten that the Lord is able to do all things according to his will, for the children of men, if it so be that they exercise faith in him? Wherefore, let us be faithful to him.

If I exercise faith in the Lord and am faithful to Him, then He is able to do all things according to His will for me.

10:17 And it came to pass after I, Nephi, having heard all the words of my father, concerning the things which he saw in a vision, and also the things which he spake by the power of the Holy Ghost, which power he received by faith on the Son of God—and the Son of God was the Messiah who should come—I, Nephi, was desirous also that I might see, and hear, and know of these things, by the power of the Holy Ghost, which is the gift of God unto all those who diligently seek him, as well in times of old as in the time that he should manifest himself unto the children of men.

> 18 For he is the same yesterday, to-day, and forever; and the way is prepared for all men from the foundation of the world, if it so be that they repent and come unto him.

If I exercise faith in the Son of God, then I will speak by the power of the Holy Ghost.

If I diligently seek the Holy Ghost, then He will be given to me as a gift of God.

If I will listen to the Word of God spoken by the power of the Holy Ghost with the intent to learn, then a desire will be born in me to see, hear, and know of the truth by the power of the Holy Ghost.

As I come to know the truth by the power of the Holy Ghost, if I desire to repent and come to God, then the way is prepared for me to return through Jesus Christ.

> **10:19** For he that diligently seeketh shall find; and the mysteries of God shall be unfolded unto them, by the power of the Holy Ghost, as well in these times as in times of old, and as well in times of old as in times to come; wherefore, the course of the Lord is one eternal round.

If I diligently seek God, then I will find Him, and His mysteries will be revealed to me by the power of the Holy Ghost.

> **10:20** Therefore remember, O man, for all thy doings thou shalt be brought into judgment.

I will be judged according to all my works.

10:21 Wherefore, if ye have sought to do wickedly in the days of your probation, then ye are found unclean before the judgment-seat of God; and no unclean thing can dwell with God; wherefore, ye must be cast off forever.

If I seek to do wickedness all my life, then I will be unclean at the judgment seat of God, and I will be cast off forever, for no unclean thing can dwell with God.

11:1 For it came to pass after I had desired to know the things that my father had seen, and believing that the Lord was able to make them known unto me, as I sat pondering in mine heart I was caught away in the Spirit of the Lord, yea, into an exceedingly high mountain, which I never had before seen, and upon which I never had before set my foot.

If I desire to know the truth of the things that I have been taught, and believe the Lord is able to make the truth known to me, and if I will take time to ponder on these things, then I will be taught by the Spirit of the Lord and learn.

11:36 And it came to pass that I saw and bear record, that the great and spacious building was the pride of the world; and it fell, and the fall thereof was exceedingly great. And the angel of the Lord spake unto me again, saying: Thus shall be the destruction of all nations, kindreds, tongues, and people, that shall fight against the twelve apostles of the Lamb.

If nations, kindred, tongues, and people fight against the twelve Apostles of Jesus Christ, then those who fight will be destroyed.

Likewise, if I fight against the twelve Apostles of Jesus Christ, then I will be destroyed.

12:10 And these twelve ministers whom thou beholdest shall judge thy seed. And, behold, they are righteous forever; for because of their faith in the Lamb of God their garments are made white in his blood.
11 And the angel said unto me: Look! And I looked, and beheld three generations pass away in righteousness; and their garments were white even like unto the Lamb of God. And the angel said unto me: These are made white in the blood of the Lamb, because of their faith in him.

If I exercise faith in Jesus Christ, then I will be made clean in His blood.

12:19 And while the angel spake these words, I beheld and saw that the seed of my brethren did contend against my seed, according to the word of the angel; and because of the pride of my seed, and the temptations of the devil, I beheld that the seed of my brethren did overpower the people of my seed.

If I am full of pride and succumb to the temptations of the devil, then I will be overpowered by him.

13:37 And blessed are they who shall seek to bring forth my Zion at that day, for they shall have the gift and the power of the Holy Ghost; and if they endure unto the end they shall be lifted up at the last day, and shall be saved in the everlasting kingdom of the Lamb; and whoso shall publish peace, yea, tidings of great joy, how beautiful upon the mountains shall they be.

1 Nephi 13:37 may, at first glance, seem to be written only to those who assist in bringing forth the *Book of Mormon*, such as Joseph Smith, or Oliver Cowdery. I believe that the promises contained in this verse can be realized by anyone who will share with others the glorious news of the restoration. Are they not seeking to bring forth the Lord's Zion?

If I seek to bring forth the Lord's Zion, then I will have the gift and power of the Holy Ghost.

If I endure to the end of my life, then I will be lifted up at the last day and saved in the kingdom of God.

If I share the gospel of peace and great joy, then my countenance will be one of Christlike beauty and light.

> **13:40** And the angel spake unto me, saying: These last records, which thou hast seen among the Gentiles, shall establish the truth of the first, which are of the twelve apostles of the Lamb, and shall make known the plain and precious things which have been taken away from them; and shall make known to all kindreds, tongues, and people, that the Lamb of God is the Son of the Eternal Father, and the Savior of the world; and that all men must come unto him, or they cannot be saved.

The Book of Mormon's prime purpose is "the convincing of the Jew and Gentile that JESUS is the CHRIST, the ETERNAL GOD" and that salvation is in Him (see the *Book of Mormon* title page).

If I do not come to Christ, then I cannot be saved.

> **14:1** And it shall come to pass, that if the Gentiles shall hearken unto the Lamb of God in that day that he shall

manifest himself unto them in word, and also in power, in very deed, unto the taking away of their stumbling blocks—

2 And harden not their hearts against the Lamb of God, they shall be numbered among the seed of thy father; yea, they shall be numbered among the house of Israel; and they shall be a blessed people upon the promised land forever; they shall be no more brought down into captivity; and the house of Israel shall no more be confounded.

If I hearken to Jesus Christ with an open heart when He manifests Himself to me in Word, power, and deed, then I will be numbered among the house of Israel, and I will be blessed forever.

14:5 And it came to pass that the angel spake unto me, Nephi, saying: Thou hast beheld that if the Gentiles repent it shall be well with them; and thou also knowest concerning the covenants of the Lord unto the house of Israel; and thou also hast heard that whoso repenteth not must perish.

If I repent, then it shall be well with me. Conversely, if I do not repent, then I must perish.

14:6 Therefore, wo be unto the Gentiles if it so be that they harden their hearts against the Lamb of God.

If I harden my heart against Christ, then woe will befall me.

15:11 Do ye not remember the things which the Lord hath said?—If ye will not harden your hearts, and ask me in faith, believing that ye shall receive, with diligence in keeping my commandments, surely these things shall be made known unto you.

If I do not harden my heart, and if I ask in faith, believing that I will receive, and if I keep the commandments with all diligence, then the Lord will make known what I ask.

15:24 And I said unto them that it was the word of God; and whoso would hearken unto the word of God, and would hold fast unto it, they would never perish; neither could the temptations and the fiery darts of the adversary overpower them unto blindness, to lead them away to destruction.

If I obey the Word of God as found in the Scriptures or from the mouth of inspired leaders, and hold fast to it, then I will never perish. The temptations of the adversary will not blind me, overpower me, and lead me away to destruction.

15:33 Wherefore, if they should die in their wickedness they must be cast off also, as to the things which are spiritual, which are pertaining to righteousness; wherefore, they must be brought to stand before God, to be judged of their works; and if their works have been filthiness they must needs be filthy; and if they be filthy it must needs be that they cannot dwell in the kingdom of God; if so, the kingdom of God must be filthy also.

If I die in my wickedness, then I will die a spiritual death.

I will be judged by God according to my works.

If my works have been filthy, then I cannot dwell in the kingdom of God.

> **16:3** And now my brethren, if ye were righteous and were willing to hearken to the truth, and give heed unto it, that ye might walk uprightly before God, then ye would not murmur because of the truth, and say: Thou speakest hard things against us.

If I listen and obey the truth in order to be righteous and upright before God, then I will not grumble and be discomforted because of the truth.

> **17:3** And thus we see that the commandments of God must be fulfilled. And if it so be that the children of men keep the commandments of God he doth nourish them, and strengthen them, and provide means whereby they can accomplish the thing which he has commanded them; wherefore, he did provide means for us while we did sojourn in the wilderness.

If I keep the commandments of God, then He will give me strength, nourishment, and the means to accomplish His will.

> **17:13** And I will also be your light in the wilderness; and I will prepare the way before you, if it so be that ye shall keep my commandments; wherefore, inasmuch as ye shall keep my commandments ye shall be led towards the promised land; and ye shall know that it is by me that ye are led.

Although this particular covenant may only apply to the children of Lehi, we can apply the principle to ourselves.

If I will keep the commandments of God, then He will be my light in my personal wandering, and He will lead me towards my promised land.

> **17:50** And I said unto them: If God had commanded me to do all things I could do them. If he should command me that I should say unto this water, be thou earth, it should be earth; and if I should say it, it would be done.

If God commands, then I can do it.

> **17:55** And now, they said: We know of a surety that the Lord is with thee, for we know that it is the power of the Lord that has shaken us. And they fell down before me, and were about to worship me, but I would not suffer them, saying: I am thy brother, yea, even thy younger brother; wherefore, worship the Lord thy God, and honor thy father and thy mother, that thy days may be long in the land which the Lord thy God shall give thee.

The word "may" is interesting in this verse and many others. I think this promise to us is conditional upon the needs of the Lord.

If I worship the Lord my God, and honor my father and mother, then my days may be long in the land which the Lord has given me.

> **19:23** And I did read many things unto them which were written in the books of Moses; but that I might more fully persuade them to believe in the Lord their redeemer I did read unto them that which was written by the prophet Isaiah; for I

did liken all scriptures unto us, that it might be for our profit and learning.

If I read and study the words of Isaiah, then I will profit and learn, being persuaded to believe in the Lord my Redeemer more fully.

19:24 Wherefore I spake unto them, saying: Hear ye the words of the prophet, ye who are a remnant of the house of Israel, a branch who have been broken off; hear ye the words of the prophet, which were written unto all the house of Israel, and liken them unto yourselves, that ye may have hope as well as your brethren from whom ye have been broken off; for after this manner has the prophet written.

If I hear the words of Isaiah and liken them unto myself, then I will have hope and learn to believe in the Lord.

20:18 O that thou hadst hearkened to my commandments—then had thy peace been as a river, and thy righteousness as the waves of the sea.

19 Thy seed also had been as the sand; the offspring of thy bowels like the gravel thereof; his name should not have been cut off nor destroyed from before me.

If I obey the Lord's commandments, then I will be at peace, my righteousness will give me great power, my offspring will be innumerable, and I will not be cut off or destroyed before the Lord.

21:5 And now, saith the Lord—that formed me from the womb that I should be his servant, to bring Jacob again to

> him—though Israel be not gathered, yet shall I be glorious in the eyes of the Lord, and my God shall be my strength.

Israel will one day be glorious in the eyes of the Lord. The Lord will be their strength. I can liken this verse unto myself by remembering that if I should wander away from the Lord, as Israel wandered away, it will not be impossible for me to return and be glorious in the eyes of the Lord. This will only be possible as I desire it, and then through the strength of the Lord.

> **22:14** And every nation which shall war against thee, O house of Israel, shall be turned one against another, and they shall fall into the pit which they digged to ensnare the people of the Lord. And all that fight against Zion shall be destroyed, and that great whore, who hath perverted the right ways of the Lord, yea, that great and abominable church, shall tumble to the dust and great shall be the fall of it.
>
> 19 For behold, the righteous shall not perish; for the time surely must come that all they who fight against Zion shall be cut off.

These verses of Scripture contain several covenants to both the individual and to entire nations.

If nations war against Israel, then they will be turned one against another and become caught by their own scheming.

If I fight against the people of God, then I will be cut off.

If I am righteous, then I will not spiritually perish.

If any organization perverts the right ways of the Lord, then they shall tumble to the dust.

22:15 For behold, saith the prophet, the time cometh speedily that Satan shall have no more power over the hearts of the children of men; for the day soon cometh that all the proud and they who do wickedly shall be as stubble; and the day cometh that they must be burned.

If I am proud and do wickedly, then I will be burned when the earth is purified by fire.

22:17 Wherefore, he will preserve the righteous by his power, even if it so be that the fulness of his wrath must come, and the righteous be preserved, even unto the destruction of their enemies by fire. Wherefore, the righteous need not fear; for thus saith the prophet, they shall be saved, even if it so be as by fire.
22 And the righteous need not fear, for they are those who shall not be confounded. But it is the kingdom of the devil, which shall be built up among the children of men, which kingdom is established among them which are in the flesh.

If I am righteous, then I need not fear, for the Lord will preserve me and I will not be confounded.

22:20 And the Lord will surely prepare a way for his people, unto the fulfilling of the words of Moses, which he spake, saying: A prophet shall the Lord your God raise up unto you, like unto me; him shall ye hear in all things whatsoever he shall say unto you. And it shall come to pass that all those who will not hear that prophet shall be cut off from among the people.

If I do not listen to and obey the Prophet (Jesus Christ), then I will be separated from His people.

> **22:23** For the time speedily shall come that all churches which are built up to get gain, and all those who are built up to get power over the flesh, and those who are built up to become popular in the eyes of the world, and those who seek the lusts of the flesh and the things of the world, and to do all manner of iniquity; yea, in fine, all those who belong to the kingdom of the devil are they who need fear, and tremble, and quake; they are those who must be brought low in the dust; they are those who must be consumed as stubble; and this is according to the words of the prophet.

If I build up churches to get gain, if I build myself up to get power over others, if I build myself up to become popular in the eyes of the world, if I seek the lusts of the flesh, and of the world and do all manner of iniquity, if I belong to the kingdom of the devil; then someday I will fear, tremble, and quake, because I will know that I will need to be humbled and then consumed.

> **22:28** But, behold, all nations, kindreds, tongues, and people shall dwell safely in the Holy One of Israel if it so be that they will repent.

If I repent, then I will dwell safely in Jesus Christ.

> **22:31** Wherefore, ye need not suppose that I and my father are the only ones that have testified, and also taught them. Wherefore, if ye shall be obedient to the commandments, and endure to the end, ye shall be saved at the last day. And thus it is. Amen.

If I obey the commandments and endure to the end, then I will be saved at the last day.

2 Nephi

> **1:7** Wherefore, this land is consecrated unto him whom he shall bring. And if it so be that they shall serve him according to the commandments which he hath given, it shall be a land of liberty unto them; wherefore, they shall never be brought down into captivity; if so, it shall be because of iniquity; for if iniquity shall abound cursed shall be the land for their sakes, but unto the righteous it shall be blessed forever.

If I, or anyone who comes to this land, will serve God according to the commandments He has given, then it shall be a land of liberty. We shall never be brought down into captivity and the land will be blessed forever.

If iniquity abounds, then the land will be cursed for the sake of the wicked.

> **1:20** And he hath said that: Inasmuch as ye shall keep my commandments ye shall prosper in the land; but inasmuch as ye will not keep my commandments ye shall be cut off from my presence.

Lehi again reminds his children, and us, of the covenant. Also, this covenant is stated in both the positive and the negative; it may be that the Lord reaches more of His children this way.

If I keep the Lord's commandments, then I will prosper in the land.

If I do not keep the Lord's commandments, then I will be cut off from His presence.

> **1:21** And now that my soul might have joy in you, and that my heart might leave this world with gladness because of you, that I might not be brought down with grief and sorrow to the grave, arise from the dust, my sons, and be men, and be determined in one mind and in one heart, united in all things, that ye may not come down into captivity;
>
> 22 That ye may not be cursed with a sore cursing; and also, that ye may not incur the displeasure of a just God upon you, unto the destruction, yea, the eternal destruction of both soul and body.

If we liken the Scriptures unto ourselves, then we can take the promises made by Lehi to his sons and apply them to our own lives in our own families, and profit by them.

If I and my brothers rise above the condition in which we find ourselves, to become determined and united men, then we will not come down into captivity and be overcome. We will not bring a cursing upon ourselves and incur the displeasure of a just God, who may bring destruction of body and soul.

> **2:7** Behold, he offereth himself a sacrifice for sin, to answer the ends of the law, unto all those who have a broken heart

and a contrite spirit; and unto none else can the ends of the law be answered.

8 Wherefore, how great the importance to make these things known unto the inhabitants of the earth, that they may know that there is no flesh that can dwell in the presence of God, save it be through the merits, and mercy, and grace of the Holy Messiah, who layeth down his life according to the flesh, and taketh it again by the power of the Spirit, that he may bring to pass the resurrection of the dead, being the first that should rise.

If I have a broken heart and a contrite spirit, then the requirements of the law are satisfied in my behalf.

A broken heart and a contrite spirit evokes the thought of one who is truly sorry for sinning, one who knows deep within that past deeds have hurt others and caused Christ to suffer and bleed in atonement. This deep, godly sorrow causes people to be truly humble and penitent, and to seek forgiveness through repentance. Through repentance, the requirements of the law are satisfied for me; I can obtain mercy and be saved in the kingdom of God.

2:28 And now, my sons, I would that ye should look to the great Mediator, and hearken unto his great commandments; and be faithful unto his words, and choose eternal life, according to the will of his Holy Spirit;

29 And not choose eternal death, according to the will of the flesh and the evil which is therein, which giveth the spirit of the devil power to captivate, to bring you down to hell, that he may reign over you in his own kingdom.

Once again, Lehi elects to place both choices in front of his sons so that they can plainly see the consequences of their choices.

If I look to Jesus Christ, hearken to His great commandments, and am faithful to His words, then that choice will bring eternal life according to the will of His Holy Spirit.

If I am not faithful to His words and commandments, then my choice will bring eternal death according to the will of the flesh and the evil therein, which gives the devil power to captivate me, bring me down to hell, and reign over me in his own kingdom.

> **3:2** And may the Lord consecrate also unto thee this land, which is a most precious land, for thine inheritance and the inheritance of thy seed with thy brethren, for thy security forever, if it so be that ye shall keep the commandments of the Holy One of Israel.

If I keep the commandments of God, then all the covenants that I have entered into with Him will be fulfilled.

> **4:4** For the Lord God hath said that: Inasmuch as ye shall keep my commandments ye shall prosper in the land; and inasmuch as ye will not keep my commandments ye shall be cut off from my presence.

Another reminder:

If I keep the Lord's commandments, then I will prosper in the land.

If I do not keep the Lord's commandments, then I will be cut off from His presence.

> **4:35** Yea, I know that God will give liberally to him that asketh. Yea, my God will give me, if I ask not amiss; therefore I will lift up my voice unto thee; yea, I will cry unto thee, my God, the rock of my righteousness. Behold, my voice shall forever ascend up unto thee, my rock and mine everlasting God. Amen.

If I ask and do not ask amiss, then God will give liberally to me that which I seek.

As we read the Scriptures, we read verses that promise blessings when we perform specific actions. Then we read another verse that promises the same blessings, but with additional clauses added on to the previous verses. This verse is an excellent example. We may read, "Ask and ye shall receive," but here, the Lord reminds us that we must ask for that which is right or according to His will. With a full study of all the Scriptures, and not selective choosing of verses, we come to understand and obey the full truth and teachings.

> **5:20** Wherefore, the word of the Lord was fulfilled which he spake unto me, saying that: Inasmuch as they will not hearken unto thy words they shall be cut off from the presence of the Lord. And behold, they were cut off from his presence.
>
> 27 And it came to pass that we lived after the manner of happiness.

These verses are a fulfillment of the covenants made with Lehi and his posterity concerning both those who would not keep the commandments of the Lord and those who would. The Lord does keep His promises, to our blessing or to our destruction, depending how we choose. (See 2 Nephi 1:20, 2:25.)

If I do as the Lord commands, then I will live happily.

> **6:12** And blessed are the Gentiles, they of whom the
> prophet has written; for behold, if it so be that they shall
> repent and fight not against Zion, and do not unite themselves
> to that great and abominable church, they shall be saved; for
> the Lord God will fulfil his covenants which he has made unto
> his children; and for this cause the prophet has written these
> things.
> 13 Wherefore, they that fight against Zion and the covenant
> people of the Lord shall lick up the dust of their feet; and the
> people of the Lord shall not be ashamed. For the people of the
> Lord are they who wait for him; for they still wait for the
> coming of the Messiah.
> 14 And behold, according to the words of the prophet, the
> Messiah will set himself again the second time to recover them;
> wherefore, he will manifest himself unto them in power and
> great glory, unto the destruction of their enemies, when that
> day cometh when they shall believe in him; and none will he
> destroy that believe in him.
> 15 And they that believe not in him shall be destroyed, both
> by fire, and by tempest, and by earthquakes, and by
> bloodsheds, and by pestilence, and by famine. And they shall
> know that the Lord is God, the Holy One of Israel.

In verses 12–15, we find several covenants. They are all part of a single principle being taught.

If the Gentiles will repent and do not fight against Zion, and if they do not unite themselves with any church other than the Lord's church, then they will be saved.

If I fight against Zion and the covenant people of the Lord, then I will be destroyed.

If I believe in the Lord, then I will not be destroyed.

If I wait for the Lord, then I will be numbered among His people.

If I do not believe in the Lord, then I will be destroyed, but I shall come to know that the Lord is God, the Holy One of Israel.

The great principle being taught is one found throughout *The Book of Mormon*. Namely, if I exercise faith and come to Christ, repenting, uniting myself with the Lord's people by being baptized and receiving the Holy Ghost, keeping His commandments, and enduring to the end, then I will be saved.

> **6:17** But thus saith the Lord: Even the captives of the mighty shall be taken away, and the prey of the terrible shall be delivered; for the Mighty God shall deliver his covenant people. For thus saith the Lord: I will contend with them that contendeth with thee—

The Lord will contend with those who contend with me, and He will deliver me.

> **9:18** But, behold, the righteous, the saints of the Holy One of Israel, they who have believed in the Holy One of Israel, they who have endured the crosses of the world, and despised the shame of it, they shall inherit the kingdom of God, which

was prepared for them from the foundation of the world, and their joy shall be full forever.

If I am righteous, believing in the Holy One of Israel, and enduring the crosses of the world, then I shall inherit the kingdom of God, and my joy shall never end.

9:24 And if they will not repent and believe in his name, and be baptized in his name, and endure to the end, they must be damned; for the Lord God, the Holy One of Israel, has spoken it.

If I will not repent, if I will not believe in Jesus Christ, be baptized in His name, and endure to the end, then I must be damned.

9:31 And wo unto the deaf that will not hear; for they shall perish.

If I am deaf to the words of God, then I will perish.

9:32 Wo unto the blind that will not see; for they shall perish also.

If I am blind to the works of God, then I will perish.

9:33 Wo unto the uncircumcised of heart, for a knowledge of their iniquities shall smite them at the last day.

If I do not cut away the evil desires of my heart, then knowledge of my iniquities will smite me.

9:34 Wo unto the liar, for he shall be thrust down to hell.

If I lie, then I will be thrown down to hell.

9:35 Wo unto the murderer who deliberately killeth, for he shall die.

If I murder, then I will die.

9:36 Wo unto them who commit whoredoms, for they shall be thrust down to hell.

If I commit whoredoms, then I will be thrown down to hell.

9:37 Yea, wo unto those that worship idols, for the devil of all devils delighteth in them.

If I worship idols, then the devil will delight in me.

9:38 And, in fine, wo unto all those who die in their sins; for they shall return to God, and behold his face, and remain in their sins.

If I die in my sins, then I will remain in my sins.

9:39 O, my beloved brethren, remember the awfulness in transgressing against that Holy God, and also the awfulness of yielding to the enticings of that cunning one. Remember, to be carnally-minded is death, and to be spiritually-minded is life eternal.

If I am carnally minded, then I will die.
If I am spiritually minded, then I will have eternal life.

> **9:42** And whoso knocketh, to him will he open; and the wise, and the learned, and they that are rich, who are puffed up because of their learning, and their wisdom, and their riches—yea, they are they whom he despiseth; and save they shall cast these things away, and consider themselves fools before God, and come down in the depths of humility, he will not open unto them.

If I knock, then the Lord will open to me.

If I am wise, learned, and rich, and if these things puff me up with pride, then the Lord will not show favor toward me.

If I consider myself a fool before God, and come down in the depths of humility, then God will open to me.

> **10:13** And he that fighteth against Zion shall perish, saith God.
>
> 16 Wherefore, he that fighteth against Zion, both Jew and Gentile, both bond and free, both male and female, shall perish; for they are they who are the whore of all the earth; for they who are not for me are against me, saith our God.

If I fight against Zion, no matter who I am, then I will perish.

If I am not for God, then I am against Him.

> **10:14** For he that raiseth up a king against me shall perish, for I, the Lord, the king of heaven, will be their king, and I will be a light unto them forever, that hear my words.

If I raise up a king against the Lord, then I will perish. How can I liken this to myself today?

If I lift up myself in pride, thinking that I do not need the Lord, or if I exercise unrighteous dominion in my home, then I will perish. Am I not in essence raising myself up as a king against or in place of the Lord?

If I hear the Word of the Lord, then He will be a light unto me forever.

> **20:1** Wo unto them that decree unrighteous decrees, and that write grievousness which they have prescribed;
> 2 To turn away the needy from judgment, and to take away the right from the poor of my people, that widows may be their prey, and that they may rob the fatherless!

If I turn away the needy, deny the poor their lawful rights, prey upon the widows, and rob the fatherless, then woe will befall me.

> **25:29** And now behold, I say unto you that the right way is to believe in Christ, and deny him not; and Christ is the Holy One of Israel; wherefore ye must bow down before him, and worship him with all your might, mind, and strength, and your whole soul; and if ye do this ye shall in nowise be cast out.

If I bow down before Christ and worship Him with all my might, mind, strength, and my whole soul, then I will not be cast out.

> **26:3** And after the Messiah shall come there shall be signs given unto my people of his birth, and also of his death and

> resurrection; and great and terrible shall that day be unto the wicked, for they shall perish; and they perish because they cast out the prophets, and the saints, and stone them, and slay them; wherefore the cry of the blood of the saints shall ascend up to God from the ground against them.
> 4 Wherefore, all those who are proud, and that do wickedly, the day that cometh shall burn them up, saith the Lord of Hosts, for they shall be as stubble.

The Lord made a covenant with Nephi that his seed would be given signs of Christ's birth, death, and resurrection. Nephi taught his children that that day would be a terrible day to the wicked, for they would perish. Once again likening the Scriptures to ourselves, if we are living in the last days, and if we are still living upon the earth at the time of the Lord's second coming, should we not assume that His second coming will be just as terrible as the first to the wicked?

If I am proud and do wickedness, then the day will come that the Lord will burn me up.

> **26:5** And they that kill the prophets, and the saints, the depths of the earth shall swallow them up, saith the Lord of Hosts; and mountains shall cover them, and whirlwinds shall carry them away, and buildings shall fall upon them and crush them to pieces and grind them to powder.
> 6 And they shall be visited with thunderings, and lightnings, and earthquakes, and all manner of destructions, for the fire of the anger of the Lord shall be kindled against them, and they shall be as stubble, and the day that cometh shall consume them, saith the Lord of Hosts.

If I kill the prophets and saints, then I will be destroyed.

It is not likely for me that I would kill the prophets or the saints physically. What can I say is more likely that I would or would not do? It is more likely that I would not hearken to what they say!

If I do not listen to and obey the Prophet, Apostles, or other church leaders, then I will perish.

> **26:8** But behold, the righteous that hearken unto the words of the prophets, and destroy them not, but look forward unto Christ with steadfastness for the signs which are given, notwithstanding all persecution—behold, they are they which shall not perish.

If I am righteous when the Lord comes, then I will not perish.

> **26:10** And when these things have passed away a speedy destruction cometh unto my people; for, notwithstanding the pains of my soul, I have seen it; wherefore, I know that it shall come to pass; and they sell themselves for naught; for, for the reward of their pride and their foolishness they shall reap destruction; for because they yield unto the devil and choose works of darkness rather than light, therefore they must go down to hell.

If I am proud, foolish, yield to the devil, and choose works of darkness rather than light, then I must go down to hell.

> **26:13** And that he manifesteth himself unto all those who believe in him, by the power of the Holy Ghost; yea, unto

> every nation, kindred, tongue, and people, working mighty miracles, signs, and wonders, among the children of men according to their faith.

If I believe in Jesus Christ, then according to my faith the Lord will manifest Himself to me by the power of the Holy Ghost. I will witness mighty miracles, signs and wonders.

> **26:15** After my seed and the seed of my brethren shall have dwindled in unbelief, and shall have been smitten by the Gentiles; yea, after the Lord God shall have camped against them round about, and shall have laid siege against them with a mount, and raised forts against them; and after they shall have been brought down low in the dust, even that they are not, yet the words of the righteous shall be written, and the prayers of the faithful shall be heard, and all those who have dwindled in unbelief shall not be forgotten.

This verse contains the covenant the Lord made with the fathers of *The Book of Mormon* concerning their children's unbelief and eventual restoration to the gospel. Although this covenant may not be given directly to the Gentile convert, we should be aware of it. If we are not part of its fulfillment in bringing them the gospel, then we can be aware of and watch for its fulfillment. This verse has direct impact on those who are children of Lehi. As they repent and are baptized, these blessings will be made manifest in their lives.

Although many of the children of Lehi do not believe and have been smitten by the Gentiles, the Lord God will not forget them.

26:32 And again, the Lord God hath commanded that men should not murder; that they should not lie; that they should not steal; that they should not take the name of the Lord their God in vain; that they should not envy; that they should not have malice; that they should not contend one with another; that they should not commit whoredoms; and that they should do none of these things; for whoso doeth them shall perish.

If I murder, lie, steal, take the name of the Lord in vain, have envy or malice, contend with another, or commit whoredoms, then I will perish.

26:33 For none of these iniquities come of the Lord; for he doeth that which is good among the children of men; and he doeth nothing save it be plain unto the children of men; and he inviteth them all to come unto him and partake of his goodness; and he denieth none that come unto him, black and white, bond and free, male and female; and he remembereth the heathen; and all are alike unto God, both Jew and Gentile.

If I come to Christ and partake of His goodness, then I will not be denied salvation.

27:23 For behold, I am God; and I am a God of miracles; and I will show unto the world that I am the same yesterday, today, and forever; and I work not among the children of men save it be according to their faith.

If I exercise faith in God, then He will work with me.

28:17 But behold, if the inhabitants of the earth shall repent of their wickedness and abominations they shall not be destroyed, saith the Lord of Hosts.

If I will repent of my wickedness and abominations, then I will not be destroyed.

28:24 Therefore, wo be unto him that is at ease in Zion!
25 Wo be unto him that crieth: All is well!
26 Yea, wo be unto him that hearkeneth unto the precepts of men, and denieth the power of God, and the gift of the Holy Ghost!
27 Yea, wo be unto him that saith: We have received, and we need no more!
28 And in fine, wo unto all those who tremble, and are angry because of the truth of God! For behold, he that is built upon the rock receiveth it with gladness; and he that is built upon a sandy foundation trembleth lest he shall fall.
29 Wo be unto him that shall say: We have received the word of God, and we need no more of the word of God, for we have enough!
30 For behold, thus saith the Lord God: I will give unto the children of men line upon line, precept upon precept, here a little and there a little; and blessed are those who hearken unto my precepts, and lend an ear unto my counsel, for they shall learn wisdom; for unto him that receiveth I will give more; and from them that shall say, We have enough, from them shall be taken away even that which they have.

In verses 24–29, a woe, or calamity, is pronounced against many people who live in the latter days because of what they do or say.

If I am at ease in Zion, crying "all is well," obeying the precepts of men, and denying the power of God and the gift of the Holy Ghost, then woe will befall me.

If I am built on the rock of Christ, then I will receive the truth with gladness, but if I am built on a sandy foundation, then I will fall!

If I say "I have enough," then the Lord will take away what I have.

If I hearken to the Lord's precepts and listen to His counsel, then I will learn wisdom, and more wisdom will be given.

> **28:31** Cursed is he that putteth his trust in man, or maketh flesh his arm, or shall hearken unto the precepts of men, save their precepts shall be given by the power of the Holy Ghost.

If I put my trust in people, making man my strength, or hearken to the precepts of men, then I will be cursed.

> **28:32** Wo be unto the Gentiles, saith the Lord God of Hosts! For notwithstanding I shall lengthen out mine arm unto them from day to day, they will deny me; nevertheless, I will be merciful unto them, saith the Lord God, if they will repent and come unto me; for mine arm is lengthened out all the day long, saith the Lord God of Hosts.

If I will repent and come to Christ, then He will be merciful to me, for His arm is lengthened out all the day to receive those who come.

Chapter 30 appears to be a covenant that the Lord has made with all the peoples of the earth concerning events that will take place when *The Book of Mormon* comes forth in fulfillment of the covenant made with Lehi and prophets after him.

Many Gentiles will believe in *The Book of Mormon*. The Gentiles will carry the gospel message to Lehi's seed. The remnant of Lehi's seed will learn who they are and come to know their ancestors; they will come to know Christ, and become a pure and delightsome people. The gathering of Israel will commence, the millennium will be ushered in, all things will be revealed, and Satan will have no more power over the children of men for a long time.

> **30:1** And now behold, my beloved brethren, I would speak unto you; for I, Nephi, would not suffer that ye should suppose that ye are more righteous than the Gentiles shall be. For behold, except ye shall keep the commandments of God ye shall all likewise perish; and because of the words which have been spoken ye need not suppose that the Gentiles are utterly destroyed.

If I do not keep the commandments of God, then I will perish.

> **30:2** For behold, I say unto you that as many of the Gentiles as will repent are the covenant people of the Lord; and as many of the Jews as will not repent shall be cast off; for the Lord covenanteth with none save it be with them that repent and believe in his Son, who is the Holy One of Israel.

This verse is an important one to keep in mind when covenants are discussed. Nephi teaches, "The Lord covenanteth with none save it be with them that repent and believe in His Son."

If I, a Gentile, will repent, then I will become part of the covenant people of the Lord.

If I, a Jew, do not repent, then I will be cast off.

> **30:5** And the gospel of Jesus Christ shall be declared among
> them; wherefore, they shall be restored unto the knowledge of
> their fathers, and also to the knowledge of Jesus Christ, which
> was had among their fathers.
> 6 And then shall they rejoice; for they shall know that it is a
> blessing unto them from the hand of God; and their scales of
> darkness shall begin to fall from their eyes; and many
> generations shall not pass away among them, save they shall be
> a pure and a delightsome people.

If the descendants of Lehi accept the gospel of Jesus Christ, then they will be restored to the knowledge of their fathers, and to knowledge of Jesus Christ. The darkness of sin in their eyes will be replaced by the light of Christ, and they will become a pure and delightsome people.

This covenant can be likened unto all: All who accept the gospel will come to know Jesus Christ; they will also come to know their fathers as they become converted to doing their family history research. The darkness of sin in their eyes will also be replaced by the light of Christ, and they, too, will become a pure and delightsome people.

> **30:7** And it shall come to pass that the Jews which are
> scattered also shall begin to believe in Christ; and they shall

begin to gather in upon the face of the land; and as many as shall believe in Christ shall also become a delightsome people.

If the Jews will believe in Jesus Christ, then they will become a delightsome people.

31:12 And also, the voice of the Son came unto me, saying: He that is baptized in my name, to him will the Father give the Holy Ghost, like unto me; wherefore, follow me, and do the things which ye have seen me do.

If I am baptized in the name of Jesus Christ, then the Father will endow me with the Holy Ghost.

An outward manifestation of this inner conversion and endowment will be shown by my works. I will follow Jesus and do the things that I have seen Him do.

31:13 Wherefore, my beloved brethren, I know that if ye shall follow the Son, with full purpose of heart, acting no hypocrisy and no deception before God, but with real intent, repenting of your sins, witnessing unto the Father that ye are willing to take upon you the name of Christ, by baptism—yea, by following your Lord and your Savior down into the water, according to his word, behold, then shall ye receive the Holy Ghost; yea, then cometh the baptism of fire and of the Holy Ghost; and then can ye speak with the tongue of angels, and shout praises unto the Holy One of Israel.

If I follow Jesus Christ with all my heart, with sincere repentance and baptism, and without hypocrisy and deceit, then I will receive the Holy Ghost and the baptism of fire, and then I will be able to speak with the tongue of angels, shouting praises to the Holy One of Israel.

> **31:14** But, behold, my beloved brethren, thus came the voice of the Son unto me, saying: After ye have repented of your sins, and witnessed unto the Father that ye are willing to keep my commandments, by the baptism of water, and have received the baptism of fire and of the Holy Ghost, and can speak with a new tongue, yea, even with the tongue of angels, and after this should deny me, it would have been better for you that ye had not known me.

This covenant is written as a warning to those who are received in baptism.

If I should deny my Savior after repenting of my sins and witnessing to the Father that I am willing to keep His commandments by being baptized by water and of fire and the Holy Ghost, then it would have been better for me that I had not known Him.

> **31:15** And I heard a voice from the Father, saying: Yea, the words of my Beloved are true and faithful. He that endureth to the end, the same shall be saved.
>
> 16 And now, my beloved brethren, I know by this that unless a man shall endure to the end, in following the example of the Son of the living God, he cannot be saved.

As God spoke to Nephi: If I endure to the end in following the example of the Son of the living God, then I will be saved.

31:17 Wherefore, do the things which I have told you I have seen that your Lord and your Redeemer should do; for, for this cause have they been shown unto me, that ye might know the gate by which ye should enter. For the gate by which ye should enter is repentance and baptism by water; and then cometh a remission of your sins by fire and by the Holy Ghost.

18 And then are ye in this strait and narrow path which leads to eternal life; yea, ye have entered in by the gate; ye have done according to the commandments of the Father and the Son; and ye have received the Holy Ghost, which witnesses of the Father and the Son, unto the fulfilling of the promise which he hath made, that if ye entered in by the way ye should receive.

If I do as my Redeemer has done, then I will know that I need to repent and be baptized. If I do this, then I will receive a remission of sins and receive the Holy Ghost. In following Jesus Christ, I will be on the "strait and narrow path" that leads to eternal life.

31:20 Wherefore, ye must press forward with a steadfastness in Christ, having a perfect brightness of hope, and a love of God and of all men. Wherefore, if ye shall press forward, feasting upon the word of Christ, and endure to the end, behold, thus saith the Father: Ye shall have eternal life.

If I press forward, feast upon the words of Christ, and endure to the end, then I will have eternal life.

32:2 Do ye not remember that I said unto you that after ye had received the Holy Ghost ye could speak with the tongue of angels? And now, how could ye speak with the tongue of angels save it were by the Holy Ghost?

If I receive the Holy Ghost, then I am able to speak with the tongue of angels.

32:3 Angels speak by the power of the Holy Ghost; wherefore, they speak the words of Christ. Wherefore, I said unto you, feast upon the words of Christ; for behold, the words of Christ will tell you all things what ye should do.

If I feast upon the words of Christ, then I will learn all things that I should do.

32:4 Wherefore, now after I have spoken these words, if ye cannot understand them it will be because ye ask not, neither do ye knock; wherefore, ye are not brought into the light, but must perish in the dark.

If I do not ask to understand the words of the prophets, then I will not be brought into the light, but will instead perish in the dark.

32:5 For behold, again I say unto you that if ye will enter in by the way, and receive the Holy Ghost, it will show unto you all things what ye should do.

If I will enter in through Jesus Christ and receive the Holy Ghost, then He will show to me all the things I should do.

32:9 But behold, I say unto you that ye must pray always, and not faint; that ye must not perform any thing unto the Lord save in the first place ye shall pray unto the Father in the name of Christ, that he will consecrate thy performance unto thee, that thy performance may be for the welfare of thy soul.

If I always pray, do not grow weary of praying, and do not do anything in the name of the Lord without first praying to the Father in the name of Christ, then He will consecrate my works and deeds for the welfare of my soul.

33:1 And now I, Nephi, cannot write all the things which were taught among my people; neither am I mighty in writing, like unto speaking; for when a man speaketh by the power of the Holy Ghost the power of the Holy Ghost carrieth it unto the hearts of the children of men.

If I speak by the power of the Holy Ghost, then the power of the Holy Ghost will carry it into the hearts of God's children.

33:3 But I, Nephi, have written what I have written, and I esteem it as of great worth, and especially unto my people. For I pray continually for them by day, and mine eyes water my pillow by night, because of them; and I cry unto my God in faith, and I know that he will hear my cry.

If I pray to the Lord with faith, then He will hear my prayer.

33:10 And now, my beloved brethren, and also Jew, and all ye ends of the earth, hearken unto these words and believe in Christ; and if ye believe not in these words believe in Christ. And if ye shall believe in Christ ye will believe in these words,

> for they are the words of Christ, and he hath given them unto me; and they teach all men that they should do good.

If I will hearken to the words written in *The Book of Mormon* and believe in Christ, then I will learn that I must do good in this life.

If I do not believe in these words but I believe in Christ, then I will learn to believe in these words, for they are the words of Christ.

Jacob

1:7 Wherefore we labored diligently among our people, that we might persuade them to come unto Christ, and partake of the goodness of God, that they might enter into his rest, lest by any means he should swear in his wrath they should not enter in, as in the provocation in the days of temptation while the children of Israel were in the wilderness.

If I come to Christ and partake of His goodness, then I will enter into His rest.

1:19 And we did magnify our office unto the Lord, taking upon us the responsibility, answering the sins of the people upon our own heads if we did not teach them the word of God with all diligence; wherefore, by laboring with our might their blood might not come upon our garments; otherwise their blood would come upon our garments, and we would not be found spotless at the last day.

If I labor with all my might and with all diligence to teach God's children His Word, then their sins will not be laid to my charge, and I will be found spotless at the last day.

> **2:17** Think of your brethren like unto yourselves, and be familiar with all and free with your substance, that they may be rich like unto you.

If I desire that my brethren enjoy the same blessings that I enjoy, and if I become familiar with all people, then I will be able to share my substance with them according to their needs. Then they will be rich (also see verses 18–19 below).

> **2:18** But before ye seek for riches, seek ye for the kingdom of God.
>
> 19 And after ye have obtained a hope in Christ ye shall obtain riches, if ye seek them; and ye will seek them for the intent to do good—to clothe the naked, and to feed the hungry, and to liberate the captive, and administer relief to the sick and the afflicted.

If I first seek the kingdom of God and obtain a hope in Christ, then I will obtain riches if I seek them. I will seek them with the intent to do good, such as to clothe the naked, feed the hungry, liberate the captive, and administer relief to the sick and the afflicted.

> **3:1** But behold, I, Jacob, would speak unto you that are pure in heart. Look unto God with firmness of mind, and pray unto him with exceeding faith, and he will console you in your afflictions, and he will plead your cause, and send down justice upon those who seek your destruction.

If I am pure in heart, looking toward God with a firm mind and praying to Him with exceeding faith, then He will console me in my afflictions, plead my cause, and send down justice upon those who seek to destroy me.

> **3:2** O all ye that are pure in heart, lift up your heads and receive the pleasing word of God, and feast upon his love; for ye may, if your minds are firm, forever.

If my mind is firm forever, then I will be able to lift up my head, receive the pleasing Word of God, and feast upon His love.

> **3:3** But, wo, wo, unto you that are not pure in heart, that are filthy this day before God; for except ye repent the land is cursed for your sakes; and the Lamanites, which are not filthy like unto you, nevertheless they are cursed with a sore cursing, shall scourge you even unto destruction.

If I am not pure in heart, if I am filthy before God and do not repent, then the land is cursed for my sake and I will not have power over my enemies (the devil and his angels).

> **3:11** O my brethren, hearken unto my words; arouse the faculties of your souls; shake yourselves that ye may awake from the slumber of death; and loose yourselves from the pains of hell that ye may not become angels to the devil, to be cast into that lake of fire and brimstone which is the second death.

If I will listen to and obey the words of the prophets, and awaken myself and my senses from a deadly spiritual slumber, then I will loose myself from the pains of hell, and will not become an angel to the devil, or die spiritually.

> **4:6** Wherefore, we search the prophets, and we have many revelations and the spirit of prophecy; and having all these witnesses we obtain a hope, and our faith becometh unshaken, insomuch that we truly can command in the name of Jesus and the very trees obey us, or the mountains, or the waves of the sea.

If I search the prophets, then I will have many revelations and the spirit of prophecy.

As I receive these blessings, then I will obtain a greater hope and my faith will grow.

As my faith grows, it will become unshakable. Then, I will be able to command in the name of Jesus, and those commands will be obeyed.

> **4:11** Wherefore, beloved brethren, be reconciled unto him through the atonement of Christ, his Only Begotten Son, and ye may obtain a resurrection, according to the power of the resurrection which is in Christ, and be presented as the first-fruits of Christ unto God, having faith, and obtained a good hope of glory in him before he manifesteth himself in the flesh.

If I am reconciled to God through the atonement of Christ, then I will rise in the first resurrection and be presented as the first fruits of Christ unto God.

If I will have faith in Jesus Christ, then I will obtain this hope of glory in Him.

5:71 And the Lord of the vineyard said unto them: Go to, and labor in the vineyard, with your might. For behold, this is the last time that I shall nourish my vineyard; for the end is nigh at hand, and the season speedily cometh; and if ye labor with your might with me ye shall have joy in the fruit which I shall lay up unto myself against the time which will soon come.

If I go into the Lord's vineyard and labor with my might, then I will have joy with the saved souls that God will bring to Himself.

5:75 And it came to pass that when the Lord of the vineyard saw that his fruit was good, and that his vineyard was no more corrupt, he called up his servants, and said unto them: Behold, for this last time have we nourished my vineyard; and thou beholdest that I have done according to my will; and I have preserved the natural fruit, that it is good, even like as it was in the beginning. And blessed art thou; for because ye have been diligent in laboring with me in my vineyard, and have kept my commandments, and have brought unto me again the natural fruit, that my vineyard is no more corrupted, and the bad is cast away, behold ye shall have joy with me because of the fruit of my vineyard.

If I labor with the Lord in His vineyard, keep His commandments, and bear good fruit, then I will have joy with Him.

6:3 And how blessed are they who have labored diligently in his vineyard; and how cursed are they who shall be cast out into their own place! And the world shall be burned with fire.

If I labor diligently in the vineyard of the Lord, then I will be blessed.

6:4 And how merciful is our God unto us, for he remembereth the house of Israel, both roots and branches; and he stretches forth his hands unto them all the day long; and they are a stiffnecked and a gainsaying people; but as many as will not harden their hearts shall be saved in the kingdom of God.

When the opportunity comes to me to hear the gospel, if I will not harden my heart, then I will be saved in the kingdom of God.

6:5 Wherefore, my beloved brethren, I beseech of you in words of soberness that ye would repent, and come with full purpose of heart, and cleave unto God as he cleaveth unto you. And while his arm of mercy is extended towards you in the light of the day, harden not your hearts.
6 Yea, today, if ye will hear his voice, harden not your hearts; for why will ye die?
7 For behold, after ye have been nourished by the good word of God all the day long, will ye bring forth evil fruit, that ye must be hewn down and cast into the fire?
8 Behold, will ye reject these words? Will ye reject the words of the prophets; and will ye reject all the words which have been spoken concerning Christ, after so many have spoken concerning him; and deny the good word of Christ, and the power of God, and the gift of the Holy Ghost, and quench the Holy Spirit, and make a mock of the great plan of redemption, which hath been laid for you?
9 Know ye not that if ye will do these things, that the power of the redemption and the resurrection, which is in Christ, will

bring you to stand with shame and awful guilt before the bar of God?

10 And according to the power of justice, for justice cannot be denied, ye must go away into that lake of fire and brimstone, whose flames are unquenchable, and whose smoke ascendeth up forever and ever, which lake of fire and brimstone is endless torment.

11 O then, my beloved brethren, repent ye, and enter in at the strait gate, and continue in the way which is narrow, until ye shall obtain eternal life.

If I repent, come with full purpose of heart to recognize the offer of salvation, cleave to God like He cleaves to me, and do not harden my heart when hearing His voice, then I will not die a spiritual death.

If I have been nourished by the good Word of God and then reject it and bring forth evil fruit, then I will be cast into the fire.

If I reject the words of the prophets and the words concerning Christ, denying the good Word of Christ, the power of God, and the gift of the Holy Ghost, and make a mockery of the great plan of redemption, then the power of the redemption and the resurrection will bring me to stand with shame and awful guilt before God. Then, according to the power of justice, I must go away into the lake of fire and brimstone, which is endless torment.

If I repent and enter in at the strait gate, which is baptism, and continue in the narrow way, which is living according to God's will, then I will obtain eternal life.

Enos

1:4 And my soul hungered; and I kneeled down before my Maker, and I cried unto him in mighty prayer and supplication for mine own soul; and all the day long did I cry unto him; yea, and when the night came I did still raise my voice high that it reached the heavens.

5 And there came a voice unto me, saying: Enos, thy sins are forgiven thee, and thou shalt be blessed.

When my soul hungers, if I will kneel down before my Maker and cry to Him in mighty prayer and supplication for my soul, then He will forgive me of my sins and I will be blessed.

1:12 And it came to pass that after I had prayed and labored with all diligence, the Lord said unto me: I will grant unto thee according to thy desires, because of thy faith.

If I pray and labor with all diligence, then the Lord will grant me my desires according to His will, because of my faith.

1:15 Wherefore, I knowing that the Lord God was able to preserve our records, I cried unto him continually, for he had said unto me: Whatsoever thing ye shall ask in faith, believing that ye shall receive in the name of Christ, ye shall receive it.

If I ask in faith, in the name of Christ, believing that I will receive, then I will receive.

Jarom

1:4 And there are many among us who have many revelations, for they are not all stiffnecked. And as many as are not stiffnecked and have faith, have communion with the Holy Spirit, which maketh manifest unto the children of men, according to their faith.

If I have faith, then I will have a close association with the Holy Spirit.

If I have the Holy Spirit, then I will receive inspiration and revelation.

1:7 And it came to pass that they came many times against us, the Nephites, to battle. But our kings and our leaders were mighty men in the faith of the Lord; and they taught the people the ways of the Lord; wherefore, we withstood the Lamanites and swept them away out of our lands, and began to fortify our cities, or whatsoever place of our inheritance.

If I am a mighty man of faith, and if I teach my family in the ways of the Lord, then we will withstand our enemies, the devil and his angels, and we will sweep them away.

> **1:9** And thus being prepared to meet the Lamanites, they did not prosper against us. But the word of the Lord was verified, which he spake unto our fathers, saying that: Inasmuch as ye will keep my commandments ye shall prosper in the land.

If I am prepared, then my enemies will not prosper against me, and the Word of the Lord will be verified in me saying, "Inasmuch as I keep the commandments of the Lord, then I shall prosper in the land."

> **1:10** And it came to pass that the prophets of the Lord did threaten the people of Nephi, according to the word of God, that if they did not keep the commandments, but should fall into transgression, they should be destroyed from off the face of the land.

If I do not keep the commandments, but fall into transgression, then I will be destroyed.

Omni

1:6 For the Lord would not suffer, after he had led them out of the land of Jerusalem and kept and preserved them from falling into the hands of their enemies, yea, he would not suffer that the words should not be verified, which he spake unto our fathers, saying that: Inasmuch as ye will not keep my commandments ye shall not prosper in the land.

The Lord will not suffer that His words go unverified. As we read and study the Scriptures, we come to learn how the Lord keeps His word, whether to our blessing or our condemnation.

If I do not keep the commandments of God, then I will not prosper in the land. Each one must answer what it means to prosper.

1:26 And now, my beloved brethren, I would that ye should come unto Christ, who is the Holy One of Israel, and partake of his salvation, and the power of his redemption. Yea, come unto him, and offer your whole souls as an offering unto him,

> and continue in fasting and praying, and endure to the end; and as the Lord liveth ye will be saved.

If I come to Christ, offer my whole soul as an offering to Him, and continue in fasting and prayer, enduring to the end, then I will be saved.

Mosiah

1:2 And it came to pass that he had three sons; and he called their names Mosiah, and Helorum, and Helaman. And he caused that they should be taught in all the language of his fathers, that thereby they might become men of understanding; and that they might know concerning the prophecies which had been spoken by the mouths of their fathers, which were delivered them by the hand of the Lord.

If I learn the language of my fathers, then I will become a man of understanding. I will learn to read the Scriptures and come to know the prophecies that were given by the hand of the Lord.

1:7 And now, my sons, I would that ye should remember to search them diligently, that ye may profit thereby; and I would that ye should keep the commandments of God, that ye may prosper in the land according to the promises which the Lord made unto our fathers.

If I search the Scriptures diligently, then I will profit and learn the commandments.

If I keep the commandments, then I will prosper in the land.

> **1:11** And moreover, I shall give this people a name, that thereby they may be distinguished above all the people which the Lord God hath brought out of the land of Jerusalem; and this I do because they have been a diligent people in keeping the commandments of the Lord.
>
> 12 And I give unto them a name that never shall be blotted out, except it be through transgression.

If I am diligent in keeping the commandments of the Lord, then I will be worthy to bear the name of the Lord.

If I transgress against the name of the Lord, then my name will be blotted out.

> **1:13** Yea, and moreover I say unto you, that if this highly favored people of the Lord should fall into transgression, and become a wicked and an adulterous people, that the Lord will deliver them up, that thereby they become weak like unto their brethren; and he will no more preserve them by his matchless and marvelous power, as he has hitherto preserved our fathers.

If I should fall into transgression and become a wicked and adulterous person, then the Lord will expel me, and I will become weak; I will not be preserved.

> **2:4** And also that they might give thanks to the Lord their God, who had brought them out of the land of Jerusalem, and who had delivered them out of the hands of their enemies, and

had appointed just men to be their teachers, and also a just man to be their king, who had established peace in the land of Zarahemla, and who had taught them to keep the commandments of God, that they might rejoice and be filled with love towards God and all men.

If I keep the commandments of God, then I will be filled with love towards God and all people.

2:9 And these are the words which he spake and caused to be written, saying: My brethren, all ye that have assembled yourselves together, you that can hear my words which I shall speak unto you this day; for I have not commanded you to come up hither to trifle with the words which I shall speak, but that you should hearken unto me, and open your ears that ye may hear, and your hearts that ye may understand, and your minds that the mysteries of God may be unfolded to your view.

If I hearken to my leaders, do not trifle with their words, and open my ears, heart, and mind to the words of God, then I will begin to understand the mysteries of God.

2:22 And behold, all that he requires of you is to keep his commandments; and he has promised you that if ye would keep his commandments ye should prosper in the land; and he never doth vary from that which he hath said; therefore, if ye do keep his commandments he doth bless you and prosper you.

31 And now, my brethren, I would that ye should do as ye have hitherto done. As ye have kept my commandments, and also the commandments of my father, and have prospered, and have been kept from falling into the hands of your enemies,

> even so if ye shall keep the commandments of my son, or the commandments of God which shall be delivered unto you by him, ye shall prosper in the land, and your enemies shall have no power over you.

If I keep the commandments of God, then I will be blessed and prospered in the land, and my enemies will not have power over me.

It is important to point out that even though we may always try our best to keep the commandments, our enemies may, from time to time, hurt us or cause us pain, or even put an end to our mortal lives. Ultimately, as we remain faithful, even to the end of our life, we will triumph over them and find rest in the kingdom of God. Our enemies will never have power to prevent us from entering the kingdom of God, since only we can do that by forsaking God (see verse 33 below).

> **2:33** For behold, there is a wo pronounced upon him who listeth to obey that spirit; for if he listeth to obey him, and remaineth and dieth in his sins, the same drinketh damnation to his own soul; for he receiveth for his wages an everlasting punishment, having transgressed the law of God contrary to his own knowledge.

If I obey the evil spirit, contrary to my own knowledge, and remain and die in my sins, then woe will befall me. I will bring damnation to my own soul and receive an everlasting punishment, having transgressed the law of God.

2:36 And now, I say unto you, my brethren, that after ye
have known and have been taught all these things, if ye should
transgress and go contrary to that which has been spoken, that
ye do withdraw yourselves from the Spirit of the Lord, that it
may have no place in you to guide you in wisdom's paths that
ye may be blessed, prospered, and preserved—
37 I say unto you, that the man that doeth this, the same
cometh out in open rebellion against God; therefore he listeth
to obey the evil spirit, and becometh an enemy to all
righteousness; therefore, the Lord has no place in him, for he
dwelleth not in unholy temples.

After learning the things of God, if I should transgress and go contrary to that which I have learned, and withdraw myself from the Spirit of the Lord, then I have rebelled against God, desired to obey the evil spirit, and become an enemy to God. Therefore, the Lord will withdraw Himself from me, for He will not dwell in unholy temples.

2:38 Therefore if that man repenteth not, and remaineth
and dieth an enemy to God, the demands of divine justice do
awaken his immortal soul to a lively sense of his own guilt,
which doth cause him to shrink from the presence of the Lord,
and doth fill his breast with guilt, and pain, and anguish, which
is like an unquenchable fire, whose flame ascendeth up forever
and ever.
39 And now I say unto you, that mercy hath no claim on
that man; therefore his final doom is to endure a never-ending
torment.

If I do not repent of my rebelliousness and my willingness to serve the devil, and die remaining an enemy to God, then at the Day of Judgment the demands of divine justice will fill me with guilt, pain, and anguish. Mercy will have no claim on me, and my final doom is to endure a never-ending torment.

> **2:41** And moreover, I would desire that ye should consider on the blessed and happy state of those that keep the commandments of God. For behold, they are blessed in all things, both temporal and spiritual; and if they hold out faithful to the end they are received into heaven, that thereby they may dwell with God in a state of never-ending happiness. O remember, remember that these things are true; for the Lord God hath spoken it.

If I keep the commandments of God, then I will be blessed to live in a state of happiness, and I will be blessed in all things, both temporal and spiritual.

If I am faithful to the end of my life, then I will be received into heaven, and dwell with God in a state of never-ending happiness.

> **3:18** For behold he judgeth, and his judgment is just; and the infant perisheth not that dieth in his infancy; but men drink damnation to their own souls except they humble themselves and become as little children, and believe that salvation was, and is, and is to come, in and through the atoning blood of Christ, the Lord Omnipotent.

If I do not humble myself and become as a little child, if I do not believe that salvation is through the atoning blood of Christ, then I bring damnation to my own soul.

> **3:19** For the natural man is an enemy to God, and has been from the fall of Adam, and will be, forever and ever, unless he yields to the enticings of the Holy Spirit, and putteth off the natural man and becometh a saint through the atonement of Christ the Lord, and becometh as a child, submissive, meek, humble, patient, full of love, willing to submit to all things which the Lord seeth fit to inflict upon him, even as a child doth submit to his father.

The natural man is a man who gives in to the temptations of the physical body. He lives after the manner of men and not of God. A saint, on the other hand, is a person who becomes child-like. A saint is submissive, meek, humble, patient, full of love, and willing to submit to all things that the Lord sees fit to give.

If I give myself over to the promptings of the Holy Spirit, then I will become a saint through the atonement of Christ. I will no longer be a natural man and an enemy to God.

> **3:21** And behold, when that time cometh, none shall be found blameless before God, except it be little children, only through repentance and faith on the name of the Lord God Omnipotent.
>
> **4:3** And it came to pass that after they had spoken these words the Spirit of the Lord came upon them, and they were filled with joy, having received a remission of their sins, and having peace of conscience, because of the exceeding faith which they had in Jesus Christ who should come, according to the words which king Benjamin had spoken unto them.

A diligent study is vital because our knowledge and understanding would grow immensely if we considered the teachings of the prophets in totality, and not single verses divorced from the other verses.

If I repent and exercise faith in Jesus Christ, then I will receive a remission of my sins and be found blameless before God. I will be filled with joy and have peace of conscience.

> **4:6** I say unto you, if ye have come to a knowledge of the goodness of God, and his matchless power, and his wisdom, and his patience, and his long-suffering towards the children of men; and also, the atonement which has been prepared from the foundation of the world, that thereby salvation might come to him that should put his trust in the Lord, and should be diligent in keeping his commandments, and continue in the faith even unto the end of his life, I mean the life of the mortal body—
>
> 7 I say, that this is the man who receiveth salvation, through the atonement which was prepared from the foundation of the world for all mankind, which ever were since the fall of Adam, or who are, or who ever shall be, even unto the end of the world.

If, after I come to know the goodness of God, His power, wisdom, patience, forgiveness, and the atonement, I will trust in the Lord, be diligent in keeping His commandments to the end of my life, and continue in the faith, then I will receive salvation.

> **4:8** And this is the means whereby salvation cometh. And there is none other salvation save this which hath been spoken

of; neither are there any conditions whereby man can be saved
except the conditions which I have told you.
9 Believe in God; believe that he is, and that he created all
things, both in heaven and in earth; believe that he has all
wisdom, and all power, both in heaven and in earth; believe
that man doth not comprehend all the things which the Lord
can comprehend.
10 And again, believe that ye must repent of your sins and
forsake them, and humble yourselves before God; and ask in
sincerity of heart that he would forgive you; and now, if you
believe all these things see that ye do them.

If I desire salvation, then I must understand that there are no other conditions whereby I can be saved, save those conditions taught in the Scriptures. What are the conditions?

1. Believe in God.
2. Believe that He lives.
3. Believe that He created all things in heaven and on earth.
4. Believe that He has all wisdom.
5. Believe that He has all power.
6. Believe that I do not comprehend all that He comprehends.
7. Believe that if I repent of my sins, forsake them, and humble myself before God, and ask in the sincerity of my heart that God would forgive me, then I will be saved.

If I believe all these things, then I must do them.

4:11 And again I say unto you as I have said before, that as
ye have come to the knowledge of the glory of God, or if ye
have known of his goodness and have tasted of his love, and
have received a remission of your sins, which causeth such
exceedingly great joy in your souls, even so I would that ye
should remember, and always retain in remembrance, the
greatness of God, and your own nothingness, and his goodness
and long-suffering towards you, unworthy creatures, and
humble yourselves even in the depths of humility, calling on
the name of the Lord daily, and standing steadfastly in the faith
of that which is to come, which was spoken by the mouth of
the angel.
12 And behold, I say unto you that if ye do this ye shall
always rejoice, and be filled with the love of God, and always
retain a remission of your sins; and ye shall grow in the
knowledge of the glory of him that created you, or in the
knowledge of that which is just and true.
13 And ye will not have a mind to injure one another, but
to live peaceably, and to render to every man according to that
which is his due.
14 And ye will not suffer your children that they go hungry,
or naked; neither will ye suffer that they transgress the laws of
God, and fight and quarrel one with another, and serve the
devil, who is the master of sin, or who is the evil spirit which
hath been spoken of by our fathers, he being an enemy to all
righteousness.
15 But ye will teach them to walk in the ways of truth and
soberness; ye will teach them to love one another, and to serve
one another.
16 And also, ye yourselves will succor those that stand in
need of your succor; ye will administer of your substance unto
him that standeth in need; and ye will not suffer that the
beggar putteth up his petition to you in vain, and turn him out
to perish.

In these particular verses, Mosiah teaches us what we should be doing that would demonstrate whether we truly believe in Jesus Christ, the Son of God, and have received a remission of our sins. The Lord makes a covenant with us, promising wonderful blessings if we will live by these principles. Then, after the statement of the covenant, He gives us further examples of the nature of those whose lives fully demonstrate that they live by the covenant they have made.

If I have come to know the glory of God, known His goodness, tasted of His love, and have received a remission of my sins, then I will experience great joy in my soul.

If I will always remember the greatness of God and my own nothingness, if I will always remember His goodness and forgiveness toward me, if I will humble myself, pray daily to the Lord, and stand steadfast in the faith; then I will always rejoice and be filled with His love, retain a remission of my sins, and grow in my knowledge of Him.

As I keep my part of the covenant, then I will not have any desire to injure another. Rather, I will live peaceably and be just with all men. I will not suffer my children to go hungry, naked, transgress the laws of God, fight, or quarrel one with another. I will teach them to walk in the ways of truth and soberness, to love one another, and to serve one another. I will succor those who stand in need of my succor by giving my substance unto them.

Up to this point, the Lord has imparted His expectations of us. He now moves into a very important explanation about His feelings concerning the poor, the needy, and His expectations of us in regards to these people. Of course, it is all done in covenant form.

> **4:17** Perhaps thou shalt say: The man has brought upon himself his misery; therefore I will stay my hand, and will not give unto him of my food, nor impart unto him of my substance that he may not suffer, for his punishments are just—
>
> 18 But I say unto you, O man, whosoever doeth this the same hath great cause to repent; and except he repenteth of that which he hath done he perisheth forever, and hath no interest in the kingdom of God.
>
> 19 For behold, are we not all beggars? Do we not all depend upon the same Being, even God, for all the substance which we have, for both food and raiment, and for gold, and for silver, and for all the riches which we have of every kind?
>
> 20 And behold, even at this time, ye have been calling on his name, and begging for a remission of your sins. And has he suffered that ye have begged in vain? Nay; he has poured out his Spirit upon you, and has caused that your hearts should be filled with joy, and has caused that your mouths should be stopped that ye could not find utterance, so exceedingly great was your joy.
>
> 21 And now, if God, who has created you, on whom you are dependent for your lives and for all that ye have and are, doth grant unto you whatsoever ye ask that is right, in faith, believing that ye shall receive, O then, how ye ought to impart of the substance that ye have one to another.
>
> 22 And if ye judge the man who putteth up his petition to you for your substance that he perish not, and condemn him, how much more just will be your condemnation for withholding your substance, which doth not belong to you but to God, to whom also your life belongeth; and yet ye put up no petition, nor repent of the thing which thou hast done.

> 23 I say unto you, wo be unto that man, for his substance shall perish with him; and now, I say these things unto those who are rich as pertaining to the things of this world.

If I justify myself in not giving to those who stand in need, saying that they have brought upon themselves their own misery, then unless I repent of this attitude, I have no interest in the kingdom of God.

With a gentle, God-like reminder that we are all beggars in one way or another, He then reminds us of the covenant that we have made together.

If I call on the name of the Lord and beg a remission of my sins, then He will not suffer that I beg in vain. He will pour out His Spirit upon me and cause my heart to be filled with joy. I will not be able to express those feelings because my joy will be so great.

Then, in a sterner reminder, the Lord makes very clear, in covenant form, our (those of us who have substance to share) unmistakable duty:

If, after God has given me what I asked of Him in faith, believing that I would receive, a person asks me in faith, believing that I would give to him of my substance so that he would not perish, I judge that person and withhold my substance, then my substance will perish with me.

> **4:24** And again, I say unto the poor, ye who have not and yet have sufficient, that ye remain from day to day; I mean all you who deny the beggar, because ye have not; I would that ye say in your hearts that: I give not because I have not, but if I had I would give.

25 And now, if ye say this in your hearts ye remain guiltless, otherwise ye are condemned; and your condemnation is just for ye covet that which ye have not received.

If I say in my heart, "I give not because I have not, but if I had I would give," then I will remain guiltless.

4:26 And now, for the sake of these things which I have spoken unto you—that is, for the sake of retaining a remission of your sins from day to day, that ye may walk guiltless before God—I would that ye should impart of your substance to the poor, every man according to that which he hath, such as feeding the hungry, clothing the naked, visiting the sick and administering to their relief, both spiritually and temporally, according to their wants.

If I desire to retain a remission of my sins from day to day and walk guiltless before God, then I should impart of my substance to the poor according to what I have.

4:27 And see that all these things are done in wisdom and order; for it is not requisite that a man should run faster than he has strength. And again, it is expedient that he should be diligent, that thereby he might win the prize; therefore, all things must be done in order.

As King Benjamin closes this wonderful address he gives us some final counsel:

If I act in wisdom and do all things in order, and not give more than I have power or means to give, then I will gain eternal life.

4:28 And I would that ye should remember, that whosoever among you borroweth of his neighbor should return the thing that he borroweth, according as he doth agree, or else thou shalt commit sin; and perhaps thou shalt cause thy neighbor to commit sin also.

If I borrow and do not return what I have borrowed as I agreed, then I have sinned.

4:30 But this much I can tell you, that if ye do not watch yourselves, and your thoughts, and your words, and your deeds, and observe the commandments of God, and continue in the faith of what ye have heard concerning the coming of our Lord, even unto the end of your lives, ye must perish. And now, O man, remember, and perish not.

If I do not watch myself and my thoughts and deeds, and if I lose faith, not observing God's commandments, then I must perish.

5:4 And it is the faith which we have had on the things which our king has spoken unto us that has brought us to this great knowledge, whereby we do rejoice with such exceedingly great joy.

If I exercise faith in the words of my leaders, then I will gain knowledge and rejoice with exceedingly great joy.

5:5 And we are willing to enter into a covenant with our God to do his will, and to be obedient to his commandments in all things that he shall command us, all the remainder of our days, that we may not bring upon ourselves a never-ending torment, as has been spoken by the angel, that we may not drink out of the cup of the wrath of God.

If I willingly enter into a covenant with God to do His will and to be obedient to His commandments in all things that He shall command me all the remainder of my life, then I will not bring upon myself the wrath of God and suffer a never-ending torment.

5:8 And under this head ye are made free, and there is no other head whereby ye can be made free. There is no other name given whereby salvation cometh; therefore, I would that ye should take upon you the name of Christ, all you that have entered into the covenant with God that ye should be obedient unto the end of your lives.

9 And it shall come to pass that whosoever doeth this shall be found at the right hand of God, for he shall know the name by which he is called; for he shall be called by the name of Christ.

If I take upon myself the name of Christ and covenant with God that I will be obedient to the end of my life, then I will find myself on the right hand of God.

5:10 And now it shall come to pass, that whosoever shall not take upon him the name of Christ must be called by some other name; therefore, he findeth himself on the left hand of God.

If I do not take upon myself the name of Christ, then I will be called by some other name, and find myself on the left hand of God.

5:15 Therefore, I would that ye should be steadfast and immovable, always abounding in good works, that Christ, the Lord God Omnipotent, may seal you his, that you may be brought to heaven, that ye may have everlasting salvation and eternal life, through the wisdom, and power, and justice, and mercy of him who created all things, in heaven and in earth, who is God above all. Amen.

If I am steadfast, solid, and abounding in good works, then Christ will seal me His, and I will be brought to Heaven and have everlasting salvation and eternal life.

7:29 For behold, the Lord hath said: I will not succor my people in the day of their transgression; but I will hedge up their ways that they prosper not; and their doings shall be as a stumbling block before them.

If I transgress the laws of God, then God will not assist me, but will hedge up my way and I will not prosper. All my doings will be a stumbling block to me.

7:30 And again, he saith: If my people shall sow filthiness they shall reap the chaff thereof in the whirlwind; and the effect thereof is poison.
31 And again he saith: If my people shall sow filthiness they shall reap the east wind, which bringeth immediate destruction.

If I sow filthiness, then everything I reap will be of no worth. I will suffer a famine of all good things and will bring upon myself immediate destruction.

7:33 But if ye will turn to the Lord with full purpose of heart, and put your trust in him, and serve him with all diligence of mind, if ye do this, he will, according to his own will and pleasure, deliver you out of bondage.

If I turn to the Lord with full purpose of heart, put my trust in Him, and serve Him with all diligence of mind, then He will deliver me from the bondage of sin.

11:20 And it came to pass that there was a man among them whose name was Abinadi; and he went forth among them, and began to prophesy, saying: Behold, thus saith the Lord, and thus hath he commanded me, saying, Go forth, and say unto this people, thus saith the Lord—Wo be unto this people, for I have seen their abominations, and their wickedness, and their whoredoms; and except they repent I will visit them in mine anger.

Upon whom will the greater portion of the anger of the Lord fall? Upon those who are not His covenant children and who do not know better, or upon those who are His covenant children and who continue to commit sin and abominations?

If I do not repent, then the Lord will visit me in His anger.

11:21 And except they repent and turn to the Lord their God, behold, I will deliver them into the hands of their enemies; yea, and they shall be brought into bondage; and they shall be afflicted by the hand of their enemies.

22 And it shall come to pass that they shall know that I am the Lord their God, and am a jealous God, visiting the iniquities of my people.

If I do not repent and turn to the Lord, then the Lord will deliver me into the hands of my enemy. I will be brought into spiritual bondage and be afflicted. Then, in my sorrow, I will know that the Lord is my God.

11:23 And it shall come to pass that except this people repent and turn unto the Lord their God, they shall be brought into bondage; and none shall deliver them, except it be the Lord the Almighty God.

If I do not turn to the Lord by repenting of my sins, then I will be brought into spiritual bondage and no one will be able to deliver me except the Lord.

11:24 Yea, and it shall come to pass that when they shall cry unto me I will be slow to hear their cries; yea, and I will suffer them that they be smitten by their enemies.

If I am slow to turn to the Lord, then He will be slow to hear my prayers, and He will allow me to be smitten by my enemies. Who are my enemies today?

11:25 And except they repent in sackcloth and ashes, and cry mightily to the Lord their God, I will not hear their prayers, neither will I deliver them out of their afflictions; and thus saith the Lord, and thus hath he commanded me.

If I do not come before God in a state of penitent sorrow, then He will not hear my prayers and He will not deliver me out of my afflictions.

12:1 And it came to pass that after the space of two years
that Abinadi came among them in disguise, that they knew him
not, and began to prophesy among them, saying: Thus has the
Lord commanded me, saying—Abinadi, go and prophesy unto
this my people, for they have hardened their hearts against my
words; they have repented not of their evil doings; therefore, I
will visit them in my anger, yea, in my fierce anger will I visit
them in their iniquities and abominations.
2 Yea, wo be unto this generation! And the Lord said unto
me: Stretch forth thy hand and prophesy, saying: Thus saith
the Lord, it shall come to pass that this generation, because of
their iniquities, shall be brought into bondage, and shall be
smitten on the cheek; yea, and shall be driven by men, and
shall be slain; and the vultures of the air, and the dogs, yea, and
the wild beasts, shall devour their flesh.
3 And it shall come to pass that the life of king Noah shall
be valued even as a garment in a hot furnace; for he shall know
that I am the Lord.
4 And it shall come to pass that I will smite this my people
with sore afflictions, yea, with famine and with pestilence; and
I will cause that they shall howl all the day long.
5 Yea, and I will cause that they shall have burdens lashed
upon their backs; and they shall be driven before like a dumb
ass.
6 And it shall come to pass that I will send forth hail among
them, and it shall smite them; and they shall also be smitten
with the east wind; and insects shall pester their land also, and
devour their grain.
7 And they shall be smitten with a great pestilence—and all
this will I do because of their iniquities and abominations.

8 And it shall come to pass that except they repent I will
utterly destroy them from off the face of the earth; yet they
shall leave a record behind them, and I will preserve them for
other nations which shall possess the land; yea, even this will I
do that I may discover the abominations of this people to
other nations. And many things did Abinadi prophesy against
this people.
9 And it came to pass that they were angry with him; and
they took him and carried him bound before the king, and said
unto the king: Behold, we have brought a man before thee
who has prophesied evil concerning thy people, and saith that
God will destroy them.
10 And he also prophesieth evil concerning thy life, and
saith that thy life shall be as a garment in a furnace of fire.
11 And again, he saith that thou shalt be as a stalk, even as a
dry stalk of the field, which is run over by the beasts and
trodden under foot.
12 And again, he saith thou shalt be as the blossoms of a
thistle, which, when it is fully ripe, if the wind bloweth, it is
driven forth upon the face of the land. And he pretendeth the
Lord hath spoken it. And he saith all this shall come upon thee
except thou repent, and this because of thine iniquities.

If I do not repent, then I will be punished. What will be the punishment that will come upon me? We see all the evil that Abinadi prophesied against the people of King Noah. Could we, too, suffer some of these same afflictions?

- Will I be visited by the anger of the Lord?
- Will a calamity be pronounced against me?
- Will I be cast into prison or brought into spiritual bondage?

- Will I be smitten, driven, or slain?
- What will be my value before God?
- Will I be afflicted with heavy burdens?
- Will I be afflicted with destructive hailstorms or by famine or by insects that infest my land and devour my garden?
- Will I suffer from a terrible pestilence?
- Could I be destroyed?
- Do I listen to what the Prophets and local church leaders testify of so that I will not suffer the calamities that they warn will come upon the wicked?

12:26 I say unto you, wo be unto you for perverting the ways of the Lord! For if ye understand these things ye have not taught them; therefore, ye have perverted the ways of the Lord.

If I pervert the ways of the Lord, then woe will befall me.

12:27 Ye have not applied your hearts to understanding; therefore, ye have not been wise. Therefore, what teach ye this people?

If I do not apply my heart to understanding the Word of God, then I am unwise.

12:33 But now Abinadi said unto them: I know if ye keep the commandments of God ye shall be saved; yea, if ye keep the commandments which the Lord delivered unto Moses in the mount of Sinai…

If I keep the commandments of God, which He has delivered by the voice of His prophets, then I will be saved.

> **13:13** And again: Thou shalt not bow down thyself unto them, nor serve them; for I the Lord thy God am a jealous God, visiting the iniquities of the fathers upon the children, unto the third and fourth generations of them that hate me;

If I bow myself down to other gods and serve them, then I will make God jealous and my punishments will affect even my children.

> **13:14** And showing mercy unto thousands of them that love me and keep my commandments.

If I love the Lord and keep His commandments, then He will show mercy to me.

> **13:15** Thou shalt not take the name of the Lord thy God in vain; for the Lord will not hold him guiltless that taketh his name in vain.

If I take the name of the Lord in vain, then the Lord will hold me guilty.

> **13:20** Honor thy father and thy mother, that thy days may be long upon the land which the Lord thy God giveth thee.

If I honor my father and mother, then my days may be long upon the land that God has given me.

15:10 And now I say unto you, who shall declare his generation? Behold, I say unto you, that when his soul has been made an offering for sin he shall see his seed. And now what say ye? And who shall be his seed?

11 Behold I say unto you, that whosoever has heard the words of the prophets, yea, all the holy prophets who have prophesied concerning the coming of the Lord—I say unto you, that all those who have hearkened unto their words, and believed that the Lord would redeem his people, and have looked forward to that day for a remission of their sins, I say unto you, that these are his seed, or they are the heirs of the kingdom of God.

If I hear the words of the prophets and obey them, believing the Lord will redeem me from my sins, then I will become the seed of Jesus Christ, and become an heir to salvation.

15:22 And now, the resurrection of all the prophets, and all those that have believed in their words, or all those that have kept the commandments of God, shall come forth in the first resurrection; therefore, they are the first resurrection.

If I believe in the words of the prophets and keep the commandments of God, then I will come forth in the first resurrection.

15:26 But behold, and fear, and tremble before God, for ye ought to tremble; for the Lord redeemeth none such that rebel against him and die in their sins; yea, even all those that have perished in their sins ever since the world began, that have wilfully rebelled against God, that have known the commandments of God, and would not keep them; these are they that have no part in the first resurrection.

If I willfully rebel against God and die in my sins, then I will have no part in the first resurrection.

16:5 But remember that he that persists in his own carnal nature, and goes on in the ways of sin and rebellion against God, remaineth in his fallen state and the devil hath all power over him. Therefore, he is as though there was no redemption made, being an enemy to God; and also is the devil an enemy to God.

If I persist in my own carnal nature, and continue to sin and rebel against God, then I will be considered an enemy to God, and it will be as though there was no redemption made for me. I will remain in my fallen state and the devil will have power over me.

16:10 Even this mortal shall put on immortality, and this corruption shall put on incorruption, and shall be brought to stand before the bar of God, to be judged of him according to their works whether they be good or whether they be evil—

11 If they be good, to the resurrection of endless life and happiness; and if they be evil, to the resurrection of endless damnation, being delivered up to the devil, who hath subjected them, which is damnation—

If my works are judged good, then I will be resurrected to endless life and happiness.

If my works are judged evil, then I will be resurrected to endless damnation, being subject to the devil.

> **18:8** And it came to pass that he said unto them: Behold, here are the waters of Mormon (for thus were they called) and now, as ye are desirous to come into the fold of God, and to be called his people, and are willing to bear one another's burdens, that they may be light;
> 9 Yea, and are willing to mourn with those that mourn; yea, and comfort those that stand in need of comfort, and to stand as witnesses of God at all times and in all things, and in all places that ye may be in, even until death, that ye may be redeemed of God, and be numbered with those of the first resurrection, that ye may have eternal life—

These verses are often quoted as being our baptismal covenant. This covenant is stated in terms of what the desires of my heart ought to be if I am prepared for baptism.

If I am willing to bear the burdens of others, mourn with the mourners, comfort the sorrowful, stand as a witness of God at all times, and have a desire to enter into Christ's church, then I am prepared to enter through baptism, will be redeemed of God, numbered with those of the first resurrection, and have eternal life.

> **18:10** Now I say unto you, if this be the desire of your hearts, what have you against being baptized in the name of the Lord, as a witness before him that ye have entered into a covenant with him, that ye will serve him and keep his commandments, that he may pour out his Spirit more abundantly upon you?

If, after baptism, I will serve God and keep His commandments, then He will pour out His Spirit abundantly upon me.

> **18:21** And he commanded them that there should be no contention one with another, but that they should look forward with one eye, having one faith and one baptism, having their hearts knit together in unity and in love one towards another.
> 22 And thus he commanded them to preach. And thus they became the children of God.

If we are united, having one faith and one baptism, with our hearts knit together in love towards one another, then we will become the children of God!

> **23:10** Nevertheless, after much tribulation, the Lord did hear my cries, and did answer my prayers, and has made me an instrument in his hands in bringing so many of you to a knowledge of his truth.

This verse is good for a new missionary, particularly for one who is learning a new language.

After I have experienced much tribulation, then the Lord will hear my cries, answer my prayers, and make me an instrument in His hands to bring many to a knowledge of the truth.

> **23:15** Thus did Alma teach his people, that every man should love his neighbor as himself, that there should be no contention among them.

If I love my neighbor as myself, then there will be no contention between us.

> **23:22** Nevertheless—whosoever putteth his trust in him the same shall be lifted up at the last day. Yea, and thus it was with this people.

If I put my trust in the Lord, then I shall be lifted up at the last day.

> **24:16** And it came to pass that so great was their faith and their patience that the voice of the Lord came unto them again, saying: Be of good comfort, for on the morrow I will deliver you out of bondage.

This verse fulfills the covenant the Lord and the people made in Mosiah 24:13, which teaches us that the Lord will keep His covenants.

If I exercise great faith and patience in my personal trials, then the Lord will deliver me.

> **26:18** Yea, blessed is this people who are willing to bear my name; for in my name shall they be called; and they are mine.

If I am willing to bear the Lord's name, then I will be blessed, be called by His name, and be His.

> **26:19** And because thou hast inquired of me concerning the transgressor, thou art blessed.

If I inquire of the Lord, then I will be blessed.

26:20 Thou art my servant; and I covenant with thee that thou shalt have eternal life; and thou shalt serve me and go forth in my name, and shalt gather together my sheep.

If the Lord covenants with me that I will have eternal life, then I will serve Him, go forth in His name, and assist in gathering together His sheep.

26:21 And he that will hear my voice shall be my sheep; and him shall ye receive into the church, and him will I also receive.

These next four verses should be of particular interest to leaders as they work with the transgressor who is trying to come back into full fellowship. It is divided into two covenants.

If I, the transgressor, will hear the Lord's voice, then I will be His sheep.

If the leaders will receive me, the transgressor, into the church, then the Lord will receive me also.

26:22 For behold, this is my church; whosoever is baptized shall be baptized unto repentance. And whomsoever ye receive shall believe in my name; and him will I freely forgive.

If I am baptized, then I will be baptized unto repentance. Anyone who believes in the Lord who is received through baptism, the Lord will freely forgive.

26:23 For it is I that taketh upon me the sins of the world; for it is I that hath created them; and it is I that granteth unto him that believeth unto the end a place at my right hand.

If I believe in the Lord to the end, then the Lord will grant me a place at His right hand.

> **26:24** For behold, in my name are they called; and if they know me they shall come forth, and shall have a place eternally at my right hand.

If I know the Lord and am called in His name, then I will come forth, and will have a place eternally at His right hand.

> **26:25** And it shall come to pass that when the second trump shall sound then shall they that never knew me come forth and shall stand before me.
> 26 And then shall they know that I am the Lord their God, that I am their Redeemer; but they would not be redeemed.
> 27 And then I will confess unto them that I never knew them; and they shall depart into everlasting fire prepared for the devil and his angels.

At the sound of the second trumpet, if I never knew the Lord during my mortal life, then He will not acknowledge me and I will depart into everlasting fire prepared for the devil and those like me.

> **26:28** Therefore I say unto you, that he that will not hear my voice, the same shall ye not receive into my church, for him I will not receive at the last day.

In the next five verses, the Lord is again addressing church leaders concerning the transgressor.

If I, the transgressor, will not hear the Lord's voice, then the church leader is not to receive me into the Lord's church and the Lord will not receive me at the last day.

> **26:29** Therefore I say unto you, Go; and whosoever transgresseth against me, him shall ye judge according to the sins which he has committed; and if he confess his sins before thee and me, and repenteth in the sincerity of his heart, him shall ye forgive, and I will forgive him also.

If I transgress against God, then my church leader will judge me according to my sins.

If I confess my sins before my church leader and before God, and repent in the sincerity of my heart, then my church leader will forgive me and so will God.

> **26:30** Yea, and as often as my people repent will I forgive them their trespasses against me.

As often as I repent, the Lord will forgive me.

> **26:31** And ye shall also forgive one another your trespasses; for verily I say unto you, he that forgiveth not his neighbor's trespasses when he says that he repents, the same hath brought himself under condemnation.

If I do not forgive my neighbor's trespasses when he says that he repents, then I bring myself under condemnation.

> **26:32** Now I say unto you, Go; and whosoever will not repent of his sins the same shall not be numbered among my people; and this shall be observed from this time forward.

If I, the transgressor, do not repent of my sins, then I will not be numbered among the Lord's people.

> **27:5** Yea, and all their priests and teachers should labor with their own hands for their support, in all cases save it were in sickness, or in much want; and doing these things, they did abound in the grace of God.

If I labor with my own hands for my own support, then I will abound in the grace of God.

> **27:25** And the Lord said unto me: Marvel not that all mankind, yea, men and women, all nations, kindreds, tongues and people, must be born again; yea, born of God, changed from their carnal and fallen state, to a state of righteousness, being redeemed of God, becoming his sons and daughters;
> 26 And thus they become new creatures; and unless they do this, they can in nowise inherit the kingdom of God.

If I am born again, being changed from my carnal and fallen state to a state of righteousness, and am redeemed of God to become His son or daughter, then I will inherit the kingdom of God.

If I am not born again, then I cannot inherit the kingdom of God.

> **29:20** But behold, he did deliver them because they did humble themselves before him; and because they cried mightily

> unto him he did deliver them out of bondage; and thus doth the Lord work with his power in all cases among the children of men, extending the arm of mercy towards them that put their trust in him.

If I place my trust in the Lord by humbling myself before Him and by praying mightily to Him, then He will extend His arm of mercy towards me, and deliver me out of bondage with His power.

Alma

3:26 And in one year were thousands and tens of thousands of souls sent to the eternal world, that they might reap their rewards according to their works, whether they were good or whether they were bad, to reap eternal happiness or eternal misery, according to the spirit which they listed to obey, whether it be a good spirit or a bad one.

If I learn to obey the Lord, then I will reap eternal happiness.

If I learn to obey the devil, then I will reap eternal misery.

3:27 For every man receiveth wages of him whom he listeth to obey, and this according to the words of the spirit of prophecy; therefore let it be according to the truth. And thus endeth the fifth year of the reign of the judges.

If I obey the Lord, then I will receive my wages from Him.

If I obey the devil, then I will receive my wages from him.

4:6 And it came to pass in the eighth year of the reign of the judges, that the people of the church began to wax proud, because of their exceeding riches, and their fine silks, and their fine-twined linen, and because of their many flocks and herds, and their gold and their silver, and all manner of precious things, which they had obtained by their industry; and in all these things were they lifted up in the pride of their eyes, for they began to wear very costly apparel.

7 Now this was the cause of much affliction to Alma, yea, and to many of the people whom Alma had consecrated to be teachers, and priests, and elders over the church; yea, many of them were sorely grieved for the wickedness which they saw had begun to be among their people.

8 For they saw and beheld with great sorrow that the people of the church began to be lifted up in the pride of their eyes, and to set their hearts upon riches and upon the vain things of the world, that they began to be scornful, one towards another, and they began to persecute those that did not believe according to their own will and pleasure.

9 And thus, in this eighth year of the reign of the judges, there began to be great contentions among the people of the church; yea, there were envyings, and strife, and malice, and persecutions, and pride, even to exceed the pride of those who did not belong to the church of God.

10 And thus ended the eighth year of the reign of the judges; and the wickedness of the church was a great stumbling-block to those who did not belong to the church; and thus the church began to fail in its progress.

11 And it came to pass in the commencement of the ninth year, Alma saw the wickedness of the church, and he saw also that the example of the church began to lead those who were

unbelievers on from one piece of iniquity to another, thus bringing on the destruction of the people.

12 Yea, he saw great inequality among the people, some lifting themselves up with their pride, despising others, turning their backs upon the needy and the naked and those who were hungry, and those who were athirst, and those who were sick and afflicted.

Verses 6–12 teach us what we should look for if our churches should begin to fail in their progress. We can, however, liken this to our families.

If my family begins to fail in its progress, then I need to rid my family of any of the following sins that may have crept in:

- Pride, verses 6–8
- Wickedness, verse 7
- Being scornful to one another, verse 8
- Persecutions, verse 8
- Contentions, verse 9
- Envying, verse 9
- Strife, verse 9
- Malice, verse 9
- Iniquity, verse 11
- Being a bad example to each other, verse 11
- Inequality, verse 12
- Despising each other, verse 12
- Neglecting those who need us, verse 12

4:13 Now this was a great cause for lamentations among the people, while others were abasing themselves, succoring those who stood in need of their succor, such as imparting their substance to the poor and the needy, feeding the hungry, and suffering all manner of afflictions, for Christ's sake, who should come according to the spirit of prophecy;

14 Looking forward to that day, thus retaining a remission of their sins; being filled with great joy because of the resurrection of the dead, according to the will and power and deliverance of Jesus Christ from the bands of death.

These verses presuppose that I am forgiven of my sins.

If I humble myself and practice a "pure and undefiled religion" (James 1:27) by supporting those who stand in need of my support, imparting my substance to the poor and the needy, feeding the hungry, and being willing to suffer all manner of afflictions for Christ's sake—then I will retain a remission of my sins. In retaining, I will continue to be in a state of forgiveness.

5:21 I say unto you, ye will know at that day that ye cannot be saved; for there can no man be saved except his garments are washed white; yea, his garments must be purified until they are cleansed from all stain, through the blood of him of whom it has been spoken by our fathers, who should come to redeem his people from their sins.

If my garments are washed white, purified, and cleansed from all stain through Jesus Christ, then I will be saved.

5:31 Wo unto such an one, for he is not prepared, and the time is at hand that he must repent or he cannot be saved!

33 Behold, he sendeth an invitation unto all men, for the arms of mercy are extended towards them, and he saith: Repent, and I will receive you.

If I repent, then Jesus Christ will receive me, and I will be saved.

5:35 Yea, come unto me and bring forth works of righteousness, and ye shall not be hewn down and cast into the fire—

If I come to Jesus Christ and bring forth works of righteousness, then I will not be cast down at the last day.

5:36 For behold, the time is at hand that whosoever bringeth forth not good fruit, or whosoever doeth not the works of righteousness, the same have cause to wail and mourn.

If I do not bring forth good fruit and do not perform works of righteousness, then I will have cause to wail and mourn.

5:38 Behold, I say unto you, that the good shepherd doth call you; yea, and in his own name he doth call you, which is the name of Christ; and if ye will not hearken unto the voice of the good shepherd, to the name by which ye are called, behold, ye are not the sheep of the good shepherd.

If I do not hearken to the voice of the Good Shepherd, then I am not the sheep of the Good Shepherd.

> **5:41** Therefore, if a man bringeth forth good works he hearkeneth unto the voice of the good shepherd, and he doth follow him; but whosoever bringeth forth evil works, the same becometh a child of the devil, for he hearkeneth unto his voice, and doth follow him.

If I will hearken to the voice of the Good Shepherd, and follow Him, then I will bring forth good works.

If I hearken to the voice of the devil and follow him, then I will bring forth evil works and become a child of the devil.

> **5:46** Behold, I say unto you they are made known unto me by the Holy Spirit of God. Behold, I have fasted and prayed many days that I might know these things of myself. And now I do know of myself that they are true; for the Lord God hath made them manifest unto me by his Holy Spirit; and this is the spirit of revelation which is in me.

This is a good covenant for anyone who is sincere in his or her desire to know the truth.

If I willingly fast and pray many days to know the truth for myself, then by the power of the Holy Ghost, God will reveal the truth to me. This is the spirit of revelation.

When we want to come to know the truth, we must be willing to pay the price and make the needed sacrifice.

> **5:48** I say unto you, that I know of myself that whatsoever I shall say unto you, concerning that which is to come, is true; and I say unto you, that I know that Jesus Christ shall come, yea, the Son, the Only Begotten of the Father, full of grace, and mercy, and truth. And behold, it is he that cometh to take

away the sins of the world, yea, the sins of every man who steadfastly believeth on his name.

If I steadfastly believe in Jesus Christ, then my sins will be taken away.

5:51 And also the Spirit saith unto me, yea, crieth unto me with a mighty voice, saying: Go forth and say unto this people—Repent, for except ye repent ye can in nowise inherit the kingdom of heaven.

If I do not repent, then I will not inherit the kingdom of heaven.

5:52 And again I say unto you, the Spirit saith: Behold, the ax is laid at the root of the tree; therefore every tree that bringeth not forth good fruit shall be hewn down and cast into the fire, yea, a fire which cannot be consumed, even an unquenchable fire. Behold, and remember, the Holy One hath spoken it.

If I do not bring forth good works, then I will not be saved in the celestial kingdom of God, but will be miserable forever.

5:56 And finally, all ye that will persist in your wickedness, I say unto you that these are they who shall be hewn down and cast into the fire except they speedily repent.

If I persist in my wickedness and do not repent, then I will be hewn down and cast into the fire.

> **5:60** And now I say unto you that the good shepherd doth call after you; and if you will hearken unto his voice he will bring you into his fold, and ye are his sheep; and he commandeth you that ye suffer no ravenous wolf to enter among you, that ye may not be destroyed.

If I hearken to the voice of the Good Shepherd when He is calling me, then He will bring me into His fold.

If I do not allow any ravenous wolf to enter into the fold, then I will not be destroyed.

> **5:62** I speak by way of command unto you that belong to the church; and unto those who do not belong to the church I speak by way of invitation, saying: Come and be baptized unto repentance, that ye also may be partakers of the fruit of the tree of life.

If I come to Christ and am baptized unto repentance, then I will be able to partake of the fruit of the tree of life.

> **7:14** Now I say unto you that ye must repent, and be born again; for the Spirit saith if ye are not born again ye cannot inherit the kingdom of heaven; therefore come and be baptized unto repentance, that ye may be washed from your sins, that ye may have faith on the Lamb of God, who taketh away the sins of the world, who is mighty to save and to cleanse from all unrighteousness.

I find this verse to be very interesting in its teaching on faith. The more I am cleansed from sin, the greater my faith.

If I repent and am born again, then I will inherit the kingdom of heaven.

If I repent and am baptized, then I will be washed from my sins, and have faith in the Lamb of God.

> **7:15** Yea, I say unto you come and fear not, and lay aside every sin, which easily doth beset you, which doth bind you down to destruction, yea, come and go forth, and show unto your God that ye are willing to repent of your sins and enter into a covenant with him to keep his commandments, and witness it unto him this day by going into the waters of baptism.
>
> 16 And whosoever doeth this, and keepeth the commandments of God from thenceforth, the same will remember that I say unto him, yea, he will remember that I have said unto him, he shall have eternal life, according to the testimony of the Holy Spirit, which testifieth in me.

If I come to Christ without fear and lay aside every sin, showing God that I am willing to repent of my sins and enter into a covenant with Him to keep His commandments, witnessing to it by being baptized, then I will have eternal life.

> **7:23** And now I would that ye should be humble, and be submissive and gentle; easy to be entreated; full of patience and long-suffering; being temperate in all things; being diligent in keeping the commandments of God at all times; asking for whatsoever things ye stand in need, both spiritual and temporal; always returning thanks unto God for whatsoever things ye do receive.
>
> 24 And see that ye have faith, hope, and charity, and then ye will always abound in good works.

If I am humble, submissive, gentle, easy to be entreated, full of patience, long-suffering, temperate, and diligent, if I keep the commandments, return thanks to God, have faith, hope, and charity; then I will always abound in good works.

> **9:12** Behold, now I say unto you that he commandeth you to repent; and except ye repent, ye can in nowise inherit the kingdom of God. But behold, this is not all—he has commanded you to repent, or he will utterly destroy you from off the face of the earth; yea, he will visit you in his anger, and in his fierce anger he will not turn away.

If I do not repent, then I will not inherit the kingdom of God. He will visit me in his fierce anger, and I will be destroyed.

> **9:13** Behold, do ye not remember the words which he spake unto Lehi, saying that: Inasmuch as ye shall keep my commandments, ye shall prosper in the land? And again it is said that: Inasmuch as ye will not keep my commandments ye shall be cut off from the presence of the Lord.

If I keep the commandments, then I will prosper.
If I do not keep the commandments, then I will be cut off from presence of the Lord.

> **9:15** Nevertheless I say unto you, that it shall be more tolerable for them in the day of judgment than for you, if ye remain in your sins, yea, and even more tolerable for them in this life than for you, except ye repent.

If I do not repent, but remain in my sins, then it will be more tolerable for the wicked in the Day of Judgment than for me. Even this life will be more tolerable for them than for me.

> **9:17** And at some period of time they will be brought to believe in his word, and to know of the incorrectness of the traditions of their fathers; and many of them will be saved, for the Lord will be merciful unto all who call on his name.

If I call upon the name of the Lord, then He will be merciful to me.

> **9:27** And behold, he cometh to redeem those who will be baptized unto repentance, through faith on his name.

If I repent and am baptized through faith in the name of Jesus Christ, then I will be redeemed.

> **9:28** Therefore, prepare ye the way of the Lord, for the time is at hand that all men shall reap a reward of their works, according to that which they have been—if they have been righteous they shall reap the salvation of their souls, according to the power and deliverance of Jesus Christ; and if they have been evil they shall reap the damnation of their souls, according to the power and captivation of the devil.

If my works have been righteous, then I will reap salvation to my soul.

If my works have been evil, then I will reap damnation to my soul.

> **10:7** As I was journeying to see a very near kindred, behold an angel of the Lord appeared unto me and said: Amulek, return to thine own house, for thou shalt feed a prophet of the Lord; yea, a holy man, who is a chosen man of God; for he has fasted many days because of the sins of this people, and he is an hungered, and thou shalt receive him into thy house and feed him, and he shall bless thee and thy house; and the blessing of the Lord shall rest upon thee and thy house.
>
> 8 And it came to pass that I obeyed the voice of the angel, and returned towards my house. And as I was going thither I found the man whom the angel said unto me: Thou shalt receive into thy house—and behold it was this same man who has been speaking unto you concerning the things of God.

These two verses of Scripture show how we are blessed as we obey the will of the Lord; in other words, it is an example to us of how obedience brings blessings.

If I am obedient to the will of God, then I will be blessed.

> **10:23** But it is by the prayers of the righteous that ye are spared; now therefore, if ye will cast out the righteous from among you then will not the Lord stay his hand; but in his fierce anger he will come out against you; then ye shall be smitten by famine, and by pestilence, and by the sword; and the time is soon at hand except ye repent.

The Nephites who dwelt in the land of Ammonihah were warned that if they cast out the righteous from among them, they would bring upon themselves the fierce anger of the Lord. Applying the Scriptures to ourselves, we can take this as a personal warning.

If I cast away my personal righteousness, then I will bring upon myself the fierce anger of the Lord.

11:37 And I say unto you again that he cannot save them in their sins; for I cannot deny his word, and he hath said that no unclean thing can inherit the kingdom of heaven; therefore, how can ye be saved, except ye inherit the kingdom of heaven? Therefore, ye cannot be saved in your sins.

If I am unclean, then I cannot inherit the kingdom of heaven.

11:40 And he shall come into the world to redeem his people; and he shall take upon him the transgressions of those who believe on his name; and these are they that shall have eternal life, and salvation cometh to none else.

If I believe in the name of Jesus Christ, who took upon Himself my transgressions, then I will have eternal life. Salvation comes through no one else.

12:10 And therefore, he that will harden his heart, the same receiveth the lesser portion of the word; and he that will not harden his heart, to him is given the greater portion of the word, until it is given unto him to know the mysteries of God until he know them in full.

11 And they that will harden their hearts, to them is given the lesser portion of the word until they know nothing concerning his mysteries; and then they are taken captive by the devil, and led by his will down to destruction. Now this is what is meant by the chains of hell.

13 Then if our hearts have been hardened, yea, if we have hardened our hearts against the word, insomuch that it has not

been found in us, then will our state be awful, for then we shall be condemned.

If I do not harden my heart against the Word of God, then I will receive a greater portion of the mysteries of God until I know them in full.

If I harden my heart, then I will be condemned, for I will know nothing of the mysteries of God, which gives the devil power over me to take me captive down to hell.

12:15 But this cannot be; we must come forth and stand before him in his glory, and in his power, and in his might, majesty, and dominion, and acknowledge to our everlasting shame that all his judgments are just; that he is just in all his works, and that he is merciful unto the children of men, and that he has all power to save every man that believeth on his name and bringeth forth fruit meet for repentance.

If I believe in Jesus Christ, and come forth to repent, then He has power to save me.

This is a very important doctrine. We believe that God is omnipotent. However, we must realize that He is all-powerful only to those who repent. The unrepentant must come to God by their own will to partake of God's omnipotence. If they do not, then they show that they do not want salvation. God would cease to be God if He took away man's agency by forcing salvation upon him. (See verse 32 below.)

12:16 And now behold, I say unto you then cometh a death, even a second death, which is a spiritual death; then is a time that whosoever dieth in his sins, as to a temporal death, shall also die a spiritual death; yea, he shall die as to things pertaining unto righteousness.

If I die, having not repented of my sins, then I will also die a spiritual death.

12:32 Therefore God gave unto them commandments, after having made known unto them the plan of redemption, that they should not do evil, the penalty thereof being a second death, which was an everlasting death as to things pertaining unto righteousness; for on such the plan of redemption could have no power, for the works of justice could not be destroyed, according to the supreme goodness of God.

After having learned the commandments of God and the plan of redemption, if I should do evil, then I will suffer the second death.

12:33 But God did call on men, in the name of his Son, (this being the plan of redemption which was laid) saying: If ye will repent and harden not your hearts, then will I have mercy upon you, through mine Only Begotten Son;

If I repent and do not harden my heart, then I will obtain mercy through Jesus Christ.

12:34 Therefore, whosoever repenteth, and hardeneth not his heart, he shall have claim on mercy through mine Only Begotten Son, unto a remission of his sins; and these shall enter into my rest.

If I repent and do not harden my heart, then I will have claim on the mercy of Jesus Christ. My sins will be remitted and I will enter into His rest.

> **12:35** And whosoever will harden his heart and will do iniquity, behold, I swear in my wrath that he shall not enter into my rest.

If I harden my heart and do iniquity, then I will not enter into the rest of Jesus Christ.

> **12:36** And now, my brethren, behold I say unto you, that if ye will harden your hearts ye shall not enter into the rest of the Lord; therefore your iniquity provoketh him that he sendeth down his wrath upon you as in the first provocation, yea, according to his word in the last provocation as well as the first, to the everlasting destruction of your souls; therefore, according to his word, unto the last death, as well as the first.

If I harden my heart, then I will not enter into the rest of the Lord.

> **12:37** And now, my brethren, seeing we know these things, and they are true, let us repent, and harden not our hearts, that we provoke not the Lord our God to pull down his wrath upon us in these his second commandments which he has given unto us; but let us enter into the rest of God, which is prepared according to his word.

If I repent and do not harden my heart, then I will enter into the rest of God, which is prepared for me.

It is significant that the Lord had this phrase repeated so many times. I think He may be trying to get this important doctrine to sink into our hearts and minds. Therefore, I have not consolidated it into one phrase, but have repeated it as well.

> **13:10** Now, as I said concerning the holy order, or this high priesthood, there were many who were ordained and became high priests of God; and it was on account of their exceeding faith and repentance, and their righteousness before God, they choosing to repent and work righteousness rather than to perish;

If, through my exceeding faith, I choose to repent and work righteousness, then I may be ordained a High Priest.

> **13:13** And now, my brethren, I would that ye should humble yourselves before God, and bring forth fruit meet for repentance, that ye may also enter into that rest.

If I humble myself and repent, then I will enter into the rest of God.

> **13:18** But Melchizedek having exercised mighty faith, and received the office of the high priesthood according to the holy order of God, did preach repentance unto his people. And behold, they did repent; and Melchizedek did establish peace in the land in his days; therefore he was called the prince of peace, for he was the king of Salem; and he did reign under his father.

If I want to establish peace in my home and community, then following the example of Melchizedek in this verse will help me know what I must do to make that happen.

If I receive the Melchizedek Priesthood through the exercise of mighty faith, and by the power of that priesthood preach repentance in my family and community, and if they choose to repent, then I will be able to establish peace.

> **13:20** Now I need not rehearse the matter; what I have said may suffice. Behold, the scriptures are before you; if ye will wrest them it shall be to your own destruction.

If I lay aside, distort, or misapply the Scriptures, then I will reap destruction.

> **13:27** And now, my brethren, I wish from the inmost part of my heart, yea, with great anxiety even unto pain, that ye would hearken unto my words, and cast off your sins, and not procrastinate the day of your repentance;
>
> 28 But that ye would humble yourselves before the Lord, and call on his holy name, and watch and pray continually, that ye may not be tempted above that which ye can bear, and thus be led by the Holy Spirit, becoming humble, meek, submissive, patient, full of love and all long-suffering;
>
> 29 Having faith on the Lord; having a hope that ye shall receive eternal life; having the love of God always in your hearts, that ye may be lifted up at the last day and enter into his rest.

If I hearken to the words of the prophets, cast off my sins, and do not procrastinate the day of my repentance, if I humble myself, call on His holy name, and am watchful and pray continually; then I will not be tempted above what I am able to bear. I will be led by the Holy Spirit and become humble, meek, submissive, patient, full of love, and long-suffering. I will have faith in the Lord and a hope that I will receive eternal life. I will have the love of God always in my heart, and I will be lifted up at the last day to enter into His rest.

> **13:30** And may the Lord grant unto you repentance, that ye may not bring down his wrath upon you, that ye may not be bound down by the chains of hell, that ye may not suffer the second death.

If I seek to repent, and if the Lord forgives me of my sins, then I will not bring down His wrath upon me. I will not be bound down by the chains of hell, and I will not suffer the second death.

> **17:2** Now these sons of Mosiah were with Alma at the time the angel first appeared unto him; therefore Alma did rejoice exceedingly to see his brethren; and what added more to his joy, they were still his brethren in the Lord; yea, and they had waxed strong in the knowledge of the truth; for they were men of a sound understanding and they had searched the scriptures diligently, that they might know the word of God.

If I search the Scriptures diligently, then I will grow strong in the knowledge of the truth. I will become a man of sound understanding, and I will know the Word of God.

17:3 But this is not all; they had given themselves to much prayer, and fasting; therefore they had the spirit of prophecy, and the spirit of revelation, and when they taught, they taught with power and authority of God.

If I pray and fast regularly, then I will have the spirit of prophecy and revelation. When I teach, I will teach with power and authority of God.

17:9 And it came to pass that they journeyed many days in the wilderness, and they fasted much and prayed much that the Lord would grant unto them a portion of his Spirit to go with them, and abide with them, that they might be an instrument in the hands of God to bring, if it were possible, their brethren, the Lamanites, to the knowledge of the truth, to the knowledge of the baseness of the traditions of their fathers, which were not correct.

If I fast and pray regularly to have the Lord's Spirit with me while I fulfill my duties, then the Spirit will abide with me and I will be an instrument in the hands of God to bring His sons and daughters to know the truth, and help them come to know their erroneous traditions.

18:35 And a portion of that Spirit dwelleth in me, which giveth me knowledge, and also power according to my faith and desires which are in God.

If a portion of the Spirit of God dwells in me, then He will give me knowledge and power according to my faith and desires.

19:13 For as sure as thou livest, behold, I have seen my Redeemer; and he shall come forth, and be born of a woman, and he shall redeem all mankind who believe on his name. Now, when he had said these words, his heart was swollen within him, and he sunk again with joy; and the queen also sunk down, being overpowered by the Spirit.

If I believe in the name of Jesus Christ, then I will be redeemed.

19:36 And thus the work of the Lord did commence among the Lamanites; thus the Lord did begin to pour out his Spirit upon them; and we see that his arm is extended to all people who will repent and believe on his name.

If I repent and believe in the name of Jesus Christ, then His salvation, mercy, love, and forgiveness are extended towards me.

22:6 And also, what is this that Ammon said—If ye will repent ye shall be saved, and if ye will not repent, ye shall be cast off at the last day?

If I repent, then I will be saved.
If I do not repent, then I will be cast off at the last day.

22:15 And it came to pass that after Aaron had expounded these things unto him, the king said: What shall I do that I may have this eternal life of which thou hast spoken? Yea, what shall I do that I may be born of God, having this wicked spirit rooted out of my breast, and receive his Spirit, that I may be filled with joy, that I may not be cast off at the last day?

> Behold, said he, I will give up all that I possess, yea, I will forsake my kingdom, that I may receive this great joy.
> 16 But Aaron said unto him: If thou desirest this thing, if thou wilt bow down before God, yea, if thou wilt repent of all thy sins, and will bow down before God, and call on his name in faith, believing that ye shall receive, then shalt thou receive the hope which thou desirest.

We can learn a great lesson from the hope that King Lamoni's father had for a better life. It is good for everyone to ask the same questions:

- What shall I do to obtain eternal life?
- What shall I do that I may be born of God?
- What shall I do to have this wicked spirit (wicked desires) rooted out of my heart?
- What shall I do to receive the Lord's Spirit and be filled with joy that I may not be cast off at the last day?
- What will I give up that I may receive this great joy?

After asking the questions, we receive answers:
If these questions mirror my desires, then I will bow down before God, repent of all my sins, and call on His name in faith, believing that I will receive. Then, I shall receive the desired hope.

> **26:22** Yea, he that repenteth and exerciseth faith, and bringeth forth good works, and prayeth continually without ceasing—unto such it is given to know the mysteries of God;

yea, unto such it shall be given to reveal things which never have been revealed; yea, and it shall be given unto such to bring thousands of souls to repentance, even as it has been given unto us to bring these our brethren to repentance.

This verse contains great promises to those who desire to be great parents, missionaries, or home and visiting teachers.

If I exercise faith unto repentance, bring forth good works, and pray continually without ceasing, then I will be able to know the mysteries of God and brings souls to repentance.

26:27 Now when our hearts were depressed, and we were about to turn back, behold, the Lord comforted us, and said: Go amongst thy brethren, the Lamanites, and bear with patience thine afflictions, and I will give unto you success.

If I bear my afflictions with patience, then the Lord will give me success.

26:35 Now have we not reason to rejoice? Yea, I say unto you, there never were men that had so great reason to rejoice as we, since the world began; yea, and my joy is carried away, even unto boasting in my God; for he has all power, all wisdom, and all understanding; he comprehendeth all things, and he is a merciful Being, even unto salvation, to those who will repent and believe on his name.

If I will repent and believe in the name of Jesus Christ, then I will reap His mercy and salvation.

27:18 Now was not this exceeding joy? Behold, this is joy which none receiveth save it be the truly penitent and humble seeker of happiness.

If I am truly penitent and humble, then I will receive the joy and happiness I seek.

27:27 And they were among the people of Nephi, and also numbered among the people who were of the church of God. And they were also distinguished for their zeal towards God, and also towards men; for they were perfectly honest and upright in all things; and they were firm in the faith of Christ, even unto the end.

28 And they did look upon shedding the blood of their brethren with the greatest abhorrence; and they never could be prevailed upon to take up arms against their brethren; and they never did look upon death with any degree of terror, for their hope and views of Christ and the resurrection; therefore, death was swallowed up to them by the victory of Christ over it.

29 Therefore, they would suffer death in the most aggravating and distressing manner which could be inflicted by their brethren, before they would take the sword or cimeter to smite them.

30 And thus they were a zealous and beloved people, a highly favored people of the Lord.

If I have zeal towards God and towards men, then I will be highly favored of the Lord.

What does it mean to have zeal according to these verses?

- Be perfectly honest and upright in all things.

- Be firm in the faith of Christ to the end.

> **29:5** Yea, and I know that good and evil have come before all men; he that knoweth not good from evil is blameless; but he that knoweth good and evil, to him it is given according to his desires, whether he desireth good or evil, life or death, joy or remorse of conscience.

If someone does not know good from evil, then he or she will be blameless.

If I know good from evil, and I desire good, then good will be given to me. If I desire evil, then evil will be given to me.

> **31:9** But they had fallen into great errors, for they would not observe to keep the commandments of God, and his statutes, according to the law of Moses.

If I do not keep the commandments and statutes of God, then I will fall into great error.

> **31:10** Neither would they observe the performances of the church, to continue in prayer and supplication to God daily, that they might not enter into temptation.

If I do what the leaders of the church counsel, to continue in prayer and supplication to God daily, then I will not enter into temptation.

Along with our need to pray, supplication may include our need to study the Scriptures, both individually and in our families, and to hold Family Home Evening.

31:37 And after that they did separate themselves one from another, taking no thought for themselves what they should eat, or what they should drink, or what they should put on.

38 And the Lord provided for them that they should hunger not, neither should they thirst; yea, and he also gave them strength, that they should suffer no manner of afflictions, save it were swallowed up in the joy of Christ. Now this was according to the prayer of Alma; and this because he prayed in faith.

Can we expect the same blessings in our lives as Alma and his fellow missionaries received?

If I pray in faith, go forward and take no thought for myself, but instead give myself totally over to the service of God, as Alma and his brethren did, then the Lord will provide for me that I will not hunger or thirst, and will give me strength to withstand afflictions.

32:13 And now, because ye are compelled to be humble blessed are ye; for a man sometimes, if he is compelled to be humble, seeketh repentance; and now surely, whosoever repenteth shall find mercy; and he that findeth mercy and endureth to the end the same shall be saved.

If I repent, then I will find mercy.

If I find mercy and endure to the end, then I will be saved.

32:15 Yea, he that truly humbleth himself, and repenteth of his sins, and endureth to the end, the same shall be blessed—

yea, much more blessed than they who are compelled to be humble because of their exceeding poverty.

If I truly humble myself, repent of my sins, and endure to the end, then I will be blessed.

32:16 Therefore, blessed are they who humble themselves without being compelled to be humble; or rather, in other words, blessed is he that believeth in the word of God, and is baptized without stubbornness of heart, yea, without being brought to know the word, or even compelled to know, before they will believe.

If I humble myself, believe in the Word of God, and am baptized without being stubborn in my heart and without compulsion, then I will be blessed.

32:22 And now, behold, I say unto you, and I would that ye should remember, that God is merciful unto all who believe on his name; therefore he desireth, in the first place, that ye should believe, yea, even on his word.

If I believe in the name of God, then He will have mercy on me.

32:27 But behold, if ye will awake and arouse your faculties, even to an experiment upon my words, and exercise a particle of faith, yea, even if ye can no more than desire to believe, let this desire work in you, even until ye believe in a manner that ye can give place for a portion of my words.

This covenant is good for those who are investigating the church.

If I awaken my faculties and experiment upon the Word of God, and exercise a particle of faith, allowing it to work in me, then I will come to believe in a manner that I can make room for a portion of the Lord's Word.

> **32:28** Now, we will compare the word unto a seed. Now, if ye give place, that a seed may be planted in your heart, behold, if it be a true seed, or a good seed, if ye do not cast it out by your unbelief, that ye will resist the Spirit of the Lord, behold, it will begin to swell within your breasts; and when you feel these swelling motions, ye will begin to say within yourselves—It must needs be that this is a good seed, or that the word is good, for it beginneth to enlarge my soul; yea, it beginneth to enlighten my understanding, yea, it beginneth to be delicious to me.

This covenant continues the ideas of the previous one.

If I make room for a portion of the Lord's Word, and if I do not cast it out in my unbelief by resisting the Spirit of the Lord, then it will begin to enlarge my soul and enlighten my understanding.

> **32:37** And behold, as the tree beginneth to grow, ye will say: Let us nourish it with great care, that it may get root, that it may grow up, and bring forth fruit unto us. And now behold, if ye nourish it with much care it will get root, and grow up, and bring forth fruit.
>
> 38 But if ye neglect the tree, and take no thought for its nourishment, behold it will not get any root; and when the heat

of the sun cometh and scorcheth it, because it hath no root it
withers away, and ye pluck it up and cast it out.
39 Now, this is not because the seed was not good, neither
is it because the fruit thereof would not be desirable; but it is
because your ground is barren, and ye will not nourish the tree,
therefore ye cannot have the fruit thereof.
40 And thus, if ye will not nourish the word, looking
forward with an eye of faith to the fruit thereof, ye can never
pluck of the fruit of the tree of life.
41 But if ye will nourish the word, yea, nourish the tree as it
beginneth to grow, by your faith with great diligence, and with
patience, looking forward to the fruit thereof, it shall take root;
and behold it shall be a tree springing up unto everlasting life.
42 And because of your diligence and your faith and your
patience with the word in nourishing it, that it may take root in
you, behold, by and by ye shall pluck the fruit thereof, which is
most precious, which is sweet above all that is sweet, and
which is white above all that is white, yea, and pure above all
that is pure; and ye shall feast upon this fruit even until ye are
filled, that ye hunger not, neither shall ye thirst.
43 Then, my brethren, ye shall reap the rewards of your
faith, and your diligence, and patience, and long-suffering,
waiting for the tree to bring forth fruit unto you.

Verses 37–43 contain an amazing promise and covenant given to bestow hope and to encourage us to want to taste of the fruit of the tree of life, or, as Nephi and Lehi taught, “the love of God.”

If I nourish the Word with faith, great diligence, and patience, and while doing so look forward to the fruit that it will bear, then it will take root, producing fruit with time. I will feast upon the fruit until I am filled, and I will never hunger or thirst. Then, I shall reap the rewards of my faith, my diligence, my patience, and my forgiveness. I shall obtain everlasting life.

If I neglect the Word and do not nourish it, then it will not take root and grow. I will never be able to eat of its fruit.

> **33:21** O my brethren, if ye could be healed by merely casting about your eyes that ye might be healed, would ye not behold quickly, or would ye rather harden your hearts in unbelief, and be slothful, that ye would not cast about your eyes, that ye might perish?
>
> 22 If so, wo shall come upon you; but if not so, then cast about your eyes and begin to believe in the Son of God, that he will come to redeem his people, and that he shall suffer and die to atone for their sins; and that he shall rise again from the dead, which shall bring to pass the resurrection, that all men shall stand before him, to be judged at the last and judgment day, according to their works.

If I do the simple things the Lord asks of me and do not harden my heart in unbelief, and if I am not slothful, then I will not perish.

> **33:23** And now, my brethren, I desire that ye shall plant this word in your hearts, and as it beginneth to swell even so nourish it by your faith. And behold, it will become a tree, springing up in you unto everlasting life. And then may God grant unto you that your burdens may be light, through the joy of his Son. And even all this can ye do if ye will. Amen.

Before we will ever be motivated to make any covenant with God, we must have a desire to taste the fruit of that covenant. In other words, we must desire to reap the blessing of the covenant.

If I will plant the Word of God in my heart, nourishing it by faith, then it will become a tree springing up to everlasting life. Then, through the joy that comes of Jesus Christ, my burdens may be made light.

> **34:15** And thus he shall bring salvation to all those who shall believe on his name; this being the intent of this last sacrifice, to bring about the bowels of mercy, which overpowereth justice, and bringeth about means unto men that they may have faith unto repentance.

Jesus Christ made salvation possible for everyone.

If I believe in the name of Jesus Christ, and exercise faith unto repentance, then I will be saved.

> **34:16** And thus mercy can satisfy the demands of justice, and encircles them in the arms of safety, while he that exercises no faith unto repentance is exposed to the whole law of the demands of justice; therefore only unto him that has faith unto repentance is brought about the great and eternal plan of redemption.

If I do not exercise faith and do not repent, then I will expose myself to the demands of justice.

If I do exercise faith and repent, then the great and eternal plan of redemption will be brought about on my behalf.

> **34:17** Therefore may God grant unto you, my brethren, that ye may begin to exercise your faith unto repentance, that ye

begin to call upon his holy name, that he would have mercy upon you;

If I begin to exercise faith and repent, calling upon God in the holy name of Jesus Christ, then He will have mercy on me.

34:28 And now behold, my beloved brethren, I say unto you, do not suppose that this is all; for after ye have done all these things, if ye turn away the needy, and the naked, and visit not the sick and afflicted, and impart of your substance, if ye have, to those who stand in need—I say unto you, if ye do not any of these things, behold, your prayer is vain, and availeth you nothing, and ye are as hypocrites who do deny the faith.

If I turn away the needy and the naked, and do not visit the sick and afflicted, then my prayers will be in vain, as they will be of no value to me. I will be as the hypocrites who deny the faith.

34:29 Therefore, if ye do not remember to be charitable, ye are as dross, which the refiners do cast out, (it being of no worth) and is trodden under foot of men.

If I do not remember to be charitable, then I will be as dross, which is worthless.

34:31 Yea, I would that ye would come forth and harden not your hearts any longer; for behold, now is the time and the day of your salvation; and therefore, if ye will repent and harden not your hearts, immediately shall the great plan of redemption be brought about unto you.

Now is the day of my salvation!

If I repent today and do not harden my heart, then today the great plan of redemption will be brought about to me.

> **34:40** And now my beloved brethren, I would exhort you to have patience, and that ye bear with all manner of afflictions; that ye do not revile against those who do cast you out because of your exceeding poverty, lest ye become sinners like unto them;
>
> 41 But that ye have patience, and bear with those afflictions, with a firm hope that ye shall one day rest from all your afflictions.

This verse teaches us that when we despise those who afflict us, we sin.

If I have patience, bear my afflictions, and do not despise my enemies, then I will not become a sinner like them, but one day I will rest from all my afflictions.

> **36:1** My son, give ear to my words; for I swear unto you, that inasmuch as ye shall keep the commandments of God ye shall prosper in the land.
>
> 30 But behold, my son, this is not all; for ye ought to know as I do know, that inasmuch as ye shall keep the commandments of God ye shall prosper in the land; and ye ought to know also, that inasmuch as ye will not keep the commandments of God ye shall be cut off from his presence. Now this is according to his word.

Once again we are all reminded:

If I keep the commandments of God, then I will prosper in the land.

If I do not keep the commandments of God, then I will be cut off from His presence.

> **36:3** And now, O my son Helaman, behold, thou art in thy youth, and therefore, I beseech of thee that thou wilt hear my words and learn of me; for I do know that whosoever shall put their trust in God shall be supported in their trials, and their troubles, and their afflictions, and shall be lifted up at the last day.

If I put my trust in God, then God will support me in my trials, troubles, and afflictions. I will be lifted up at the last day.

> **37:13** O remember, remember, my son Helaman, how strict are the commandments of God. And he said: If ye will keep my commandments ye shall prosper in the land—but if ye keep not his commandments ye shall be cut off from his presence.

Alma taught this to his sons individually, so shouldn't we as well?

If I keep the commandments of God, then I will prosper in the land.

If I do not keep the commandments of God, then I will be cut off from His presence.

> **37:15** And now behold, I tell you by the spirit of prophecy, that if ye transgress the commandments of God, behold, these things which are sacred shall be taken away from you by the

power of God, and ye shall be delivered up unto Satan, that he may sift you as chaff before the wind.

16 But if ye keep the commandments of God, and do with these things which are sacred according to that which the Lord doth command you, (for you must appeal unto the Lord for all things whatsoever ye must do with them) behold, no power of earth or hell can take them from you, for God is powerful to the fulfilling of all his words.

Although Alma is talking to Helaman about the brass plates and other sacred records and objects, the same principle may apply to us and the things we hold sacred.

If I transgress the commandments of God, then those things which I hold sacred may be taken from me, and I will be delivered up to Satan.

If I keep the commandments of God and do according to His will, then no power of earth or hell can take away from me the things that I hold sacred.

37:33 Preach unto them repentance, and faith on the Lord Jesus Christ; teach them to humble themselves and to be meek and lowly in heart; teach them to withstand every temptation of the devil, with their faith on the Lord Jesus Christ.

34 Teach them to never be weary of good works, but to be meek and lowly in heart; for such shall find rest to their souls.

If I repent and exercise faith in the Lord Jesus Christ, humble myself, learn to be meek and lowly in heart, and learn to withstand the devil with my faith in Christ, then my soul will find rest.

I was taught by a wise man that if I should ever grow tired of doing good, then I have lost the Spirit of the Lord.

37:36 Yea, and cry unto God for all thy support; yea, let all thy doings be unto the Lord, and whithersoever thou goest let it be in the Lord; yea, let all thy thoughts be directed unto the Lord; yea, let the affections of thy heart be placed upon the Lord forever.

37 Counsel with the Lord in all thy doings, and he will direct thee for good; yea, when thou liest down at night lie down unto the Lord, that he may watch over you in your sleep; and when thou risest in the morning let thy heart be full of thanks unto God; and if ye do these things, ye shall be lifted up at the last day.

If I pray to God for all my support, and focus my thoughts, affections, counsels, and desires on Him, then He will direct me for good.

If I say my prayers at night before I lie down, then He will watch over me in my sleep.

When I arise in the morning, if my heart is full of thanks to God, and I do all that I have been counseled to do in these two verses, then I will be lifted up at the last day.

37:45 And now I say, is there not a type in this thing? For just as surely as this director did bring our fathers, by following its course, to the promised land, shall the words of Christ, if we follow their course, carry us beyond this vale of sorrow into a far better land of promise.

If I follow the words of Christ, then they will carry me through this life into eternal life.

37:46 O my son, do not let us be slothful because of the
easiness of the way; for so was it with our fathers; for so was it
prepared for them, that if they would look they might live;
even so it is with us. The way is prepared, and if we will look
we may live forever.
47 And now, my son, see that ye take care of these sacred
things, yea, see that ye look to God and live. Go unto this
people and declare the word, and be sober. My son, farewell.

The Lord has prepared a way for me to live with Him eternally.

If I will look to God, then I will live.

38:1 My son, give ear to my words, for I say unto you, even as I said unto Helaman, that inasmuch as ye shall keep the commandments of God ye shall prosper in the land; and inasmuch as ye will not keep the commandments of God ye shall be cut off from his presence.

Has this counsel, given by Alma and all the prophets before him, sunk into our hearts yet?

If I keep the commandments of God, then I will prosper in the land.

If I do not keep the commandments of God, then I will be cut off from His presence.

38:2 And now, my son, I trust that I shall have great joy in you, because of your steadiness and your faithfulness unto God; for as you have commenced in your youth to look to the Lord your God, even so I hope that you will continue in keeping his commandments; for blessed is he that endureth to the end.

If I am steady and faithful in my relationship to God, then I will bring joy to my father and mother.

If I endure to the end in keeping the commandments of God, then I will be blessed.

> **38:3** I say unto you, my son, that I have had great joy in thee already, because of thy faithfulness and thy diligence, and thy patience and thy long-suffering among the people of the Zoramites.

If I am faithful, diligent, patient, and forgiving, then I will bring great joy to my father and mother.

> **38:5** And now my son, Shiblon, I would that ye should remember, that as much as ye shall put your trust in God even so much ye shall be delivered out of your trials, and your troubles, and your afflictions, and ye shall be lifted up at the last day.

If I put my trust in God, then I will be delivered out of my trials, my troubles, and my afflictions. I will be lifted up at the last day.

This verse suggests to me that to whatever degree I trust God, then to that same degree I will be delivered out of my trials, troubles, and afflictions.

> **38:12** Use boldness, but not overbearance; and also see that ye bridle all your passions, that ye may be filled with love; see that ye refrain from idleness.

If I bridle all my passions, then I will be filled with love.

39:8 But behold, ye cannot hide your crimes from God; and except ye repent they will stand as a testimony against you at the last day.

I cannot hide my crimes from God!

If I do not repent, then my sins will stand as a testimony against me at the last day.

39:9 Now my son, I would that ye should repent and forsake your sins, and go no more after the lusts of your eyes, but cross yourself in all these things; for except ye do this ye can in nowise inherit the kingdom of God. Oh, remember, and take it upon you, and cross yourself in these things.

Alma is advising his son on how to overcome personal weaknesses.

If I repent and forsake my sins, leaving behind the lusts of the past, and master myself and my passions, then I will inherit the kingdom of God.

41:3 And it is requisite with the justice of God that men should be judged according to their works; and if their works were good in this life, and the desires of their hearts were good, that they should also, at the last day, be restored unto that which is good.

If my works are good in this life, and the desires of my heart are good, then at the last day I will be restored to good.

> **41:4** And if their works are evil they shall be restored unto them for evil. Therefore, all things shall be restored to their proper order, every thing to its natural frame—mortality raised to immortality, corruption to incorruption—raised to endless happiness to inherit the kingdom of God, or to endless misery to inherit the kingdom of the devil, the one on one hand, the other on the other—
>
> 5 The one raised to happiness according to his desires of happiness, or good according to his desires of good; and the other to evil according to his desires of evil; for as he has desired to do evil all the day long even so shall he have his reward of evil when the night cometh.

Alma continues to teach about the principle of restoration.

If my works are evil in this life, then I will be restored to evil, and inherit the kingdom of the devil.

Everything will be restored to its proper order. Everything will be restored to its proper frame. Mortality will be raised to immortality. Corruptible bodies will be raised to incorruptible bodies. Happiness will be restored to the happy, and misery to the miserable.

> **41:6** And so it is on the other hand. If he hath repented of his sins, and desired righteousness until the end of his days, even so he shall be rewarded unto righteousness.

If I repent of my sins and have desired righteousness until the end of my life, then I will be rewarded with righteousness.

41:7 These are they that are redeemed of the Lord; yea, these are they that are taken out, that are delivered from that endless night of darkness; and thus they stand or fall; for behold, they are their own judges, whether to do good or do evil.

8 Now, the decrees of God are unalterable; therefore, the way is prepared that whosoever will may walk therein and be saved.

If I repent and remain righteous, then I will be redeemed of the Lord, and delivered from darkness.

If I choose good, then I will stand.

If I choose evil, then I will fall.

If I walk in the ways of God, then I will be saved.

41:14 Therefore, my son, see that you are merciful unto your brethren; deal justly, judge righteously, and do good continually; and if ye do all these things then shall ye receive your reward; yea, ye shall have mercy restored unto you again; ye shall have justice restored unto you again; ye shall have a righteous judgment restored unto you again; and ye shall have good rewarded unto you again.

If I show mercy, am just, judge righteously, and do good continually to my brethren, then I will have mercy, justice, righteous judgment, and goodness restored to me as my reward.

42:13 Therefore, according to justice, the plan of redemption could not be brought about, only on conditions of repentance of men in this probationary state, yea, this preparatory state; for except it were for these conditions, mercy could not take effect except it should destroy the work of justice. Now the work of justice could not be destroyed; if so, God would cease to be God.

If I repent, then, according to justice, the plan of redemption will be brought about on my behalf. Only if I repent can the plan of mercy take effect and not destroy the work of justice.

44:4 Now ye see that this is the true faith of God; yea, ye see that God will support, and keep, and preserve us, so long as we are faithful unto him, and unto our faith, and our religion; and never will the Lord suffer that we shall be destroyed except we should fall into transgression and deny our faith.

If I am faithful to God, my faith, and my religion, then God will support, keep, and preserve me, and He will never allow me to be destroyed.

45:16 And he said: Thus saith the Lord God—Cursed shall be the land, yea, this land, unto every nation, kindred, tongue, and people, unto destruction, which do wickedly, when they are fully ripe; and as I have said so shall it be; for this is the cursing and the blessing of God upon the land, for the Lord cannot look upon sin with the least degree of allowance.

If the people who live on this land do wickedness until they are fully ripe, then they will be destroyed.

48:15 And this was their faith, that by so doing God would prosper them in the land, or in other words, if they were faithful in keeping the commandments of God that he would prosper them in the land; yea, warn them to flee, or to prepare for war, according to their danger;

If I am faithful in keeping the commandments of God, then He will prosper me in the land. He will also warn me of dangers that I may face so that I can avoid them or prepare for them.

48:25 Yea, they could not bear that their brethren should rejoice over the blood of the Nephites, so long as there were any who should keep the commandments of God, for the promise of the Lord was, if they should keep his commandments they should prosper in the land.

If I keep the Lord's commandments, then I will prosper.

49:30 Yea, and there was continual peace among them, and exceedingly great prosperity in the church because of their heed and diligence which they gave unto the word of God, which was declared unto them by Helaman, and Shiblon, and Corianton, and Ammon and his brethren, yea, and by all those who had been ordained by the holy order of God, being baptized unto repentance, and sent forth to preach among the people.

If we as a church give heed and diligence to the Word of God, as declared to us by His servants, then the church will prosper exceedingly.

This covenant can also be likened to me personally.

If I give heed and diligence to the Word of God as declared to me by His servants, then I will prosper exceedingly.

> **50:20** Blessed art thou and thy children; and they shall be blessed, inasmuch as they shall keep my commandments they shall prosper in the land. But remember, inasmuch as they will not keep my commandments they shall be cut off from the presence of the Lord.

Why did the Nephites need to be reminded of this covenant so often? Because, like us, they would forget.

If I keep the commandments of God, then I will prosper in the land.

If I do not keep the commandments of God, then I will be cut off from the presence of the Lord.

Some questions to ask myself: Am I growing spiritually? Am I progressing in life? Am I becoming more Christlike? Am I continually finding joy and contentment in service to others? If my answers are yes, then I am prospering.

> **56:47** Now they never had fought, yet they did not fear death; and they did think more upon the liberty of their fathers than they did upon their lives; yea, they had been taught by their mothers, that if they did not doubt, God would deliver them.

If I do not doubt, then God will deliver me.

> **62:51** And they did pray unto the Lord their God continually, insomuch that the Lord did bless them, according

to his word, so that they did wax strong and prosper in the land.

If I pray to the Lord continually, then He will bless me so that I will grow strong and prosper in the land.

Helaman

3:27 Thus we may see that the Lord is merciful unto all who will, in the sincerity of their hearts, call upon his holy name.

If, in the sincerity of my heart I call upon the name of the Lord, then He will have mercy on me.

3:28 Yea, thus we see that the gate of heaven is open unto all, even to those who will believe on the name of Jesus Christ, who is the Son of God.

If I will believe in the name of Jesus Christ, then the gates of heaven will be open to me.

3:29 Yea, we see that whosoever will may lay hold upon the word of God, which is quick and powerful, which shall divide asunder all the cunning and the snares and the wiles of the devil, and lead the man of Christ in a strait and narrow course across that everlasting gulf of misery which is prepared to engulf the wicked—

30 And land their souls, yea, their immortal souls, at the right hand of God in the kingdom of heaven, to sit down with Abraham, and Isaac, and with Jacob, and with all our holy fathers, to go no more out.

If I lay hold upon the Word of God, then I will be led as a man of Christ in a strait and narrow course across the everlasting gulf of misery, and land my soul at the right hand of God in the kingdom of heaven.

3:35 Nevertheless they did fast and pray oft, and did wax stronger and stronger in their humility, and firmer and firmer in the faith of Christ, unto the filling their souls with joy and consolation, yea, even to the purifying and the sanctification of their hearts, which sanctification cometh because of their yielding their hearts unto God.

If I fast and pray often, then I will become more humble and firmer in the faith of Christ. My soul will be filled with joy and consolation, and my heart will become pure and sanctified.

If I yield my heart to God, then I will be sanctified.

4:11 Now this great loss of the Nephites, and the great slaughter which was among them, would not have happened had it not been for their wickedness and their abomination which was among them; yea, and it was among those also who professed to belong to the church of God.

If we as a people, those who profess to belong to the church of God, are wicked and commit abominations, then we will suffer great loss.

What might this loss be? Unity, strength, members, youth, potential converts, but most of all—our salvation!

> **4:12** And it was because of the pride of their hearts, because of their exceeding riches, yea, it was because of their oppression to the poor, withholding their food from the hungry, withholding their clothing from the naked, and smiting their humble brethren upon the cheek, making a mock of that which was sacred, denying the spirit of prophecy and of revelation, murdering, plundering, lying, stealing, committing adultery, rising up in great contentions, and deserting away into the land of Nephi, among the Lamanites—
>
> 13 And because of this their great wickedness, and their boastings in their own strength, they were left in their own strength; therefore they did not prosper, but were afflicted and smitten, and driven before the Lamanites, until they had lost possession of almost all their lands.

If we as a people have pride in our hearts, oppress the poor, smite our humble brother, mock what is sacred, deny the spirit of prophecy and revelation, murder, plunder, lie, steal, commit adultery, contend, desert our fellow Saints, or boast in our own strength, then we will be left to our own strength, we will not prosper, and we will be afflicted, smitten and driven away.

> **4:23** And because of their iniquity the church had begun to dwindle; and they began to disbelieve in the spirit of prophecy and in the spirit of revelation; and the judgments of God did stare them in the face.
>
> 24 And they saw that they had become weak, like unto their brethren, the Lamanites, and that the Spirit of the Lord did no

> more preserve them; yea, it had withdrawn from them because the Spirit of the Lord doth not dwell in unholy temples—

If we as a people are wicked, then we will begin to dwindle. We will begin to disbelieve in the spirit of prophecy and the spirit of revelation. We will become weak, like our unbelieving brethren. The Spirit of the Lord will no longer preserve us, nor dwell within us.

If my temple is unholy, then the Spirit of God will not dwell in me.

> **4:25** Therefore the Lord did cease to preserve them by his miraculous and matchless power, for they had fallen into a state of unbelief and awful wickedness; and they saw that the Lamanites were exceedingly more numerous than they, and except they should cleave unto the Lord their God they must unavoidably perish.

If I fall into a state of unbelief and awful wickedness, then the Lord will cease to preserve me.

If I do not cling to the Lord, then I will perish.

> **5:12** And now, my sons, remember, remember that it is upon the rock of our Redeemer, who is Christ, the Son of God, that ye must build your foundation; that when the devil shall send forth his mighty winds, yea, his shafts in the whirlwind, yea, when all his hail and his mighty storm shall beat upon you, it shall have no power over you to drag you down to the gulf of misery and endless wo, because of the rock upon which ye are built, which is a sure foundation, a foundation whereon if men build they cannot fall.

If I build my foundation on Jesus Christ, which is a sure foundation, then I cannot fall.

5:17 And it came to pass that they did preach with great power, insomuch that they did confound many of those dissenters who had gone over from the Nephites, insomuch that they came forth and did confess their sins and were baptized unto repentance, and immediately returned to the Nephites to endeavor to repair unto them the wrongs which they had done.

If I speak with great power, then I will confound many.

7:17 O repent ye, repent ye! Why will ye die? Turn ye, turn ye unto the Lord your God. Why has he forsaken you?
18 It is because you have hardened your hearts; yea, ye will not hearken unto the voice of the good shepherd; yea, ye have provoked him to anger against you.

If I harden my heart and do not listen to the voice of the Lord, then I will provoke Him to anger against me, and He will forsake me.

7:23 For behold, thus saith the Lord: I will not show unto the wicked of my strength, to one more than the other, save it be unto those who repent of their sins, and hearken unto my words. Now therefore, I would that ye should behold, my brethren, that it shall be better for the Lamanites than for you except ye shall repent.

If I am wicked, then the Lord will not show His strength to me.

If I do not repent, then my enemies will be better off than I.

If I repent and hearken unto the words of the prophets, then the Lord will show His strength to me.

> **8:15** And as many as should look upon that serpent should live, even so as many as should look upon the Son of God with faith, having a contrite spirit, might live, even unto that life which is eternal.

If I look upon the Son of God with faith, having a contrite spirit, then I will have eternal life.

> **10:4** Blessed art thou, Nephi, for those things which thou hast done; for I have beheld how thou hast with unwearyingness declared the word, which I have given unto thee, unto this people. And thou hast not feared them, and hast not sought thine own life, but hast sought my will, and to keep my commandments.
>
> 5 And now, because thou hast done this with such unwearyingness, behold, I will bless thee forever; and I will make thee mighty in word and in deed, in faith and in works; yea, even that all things shall be done unto thee according to thy word, for thou shalt not ask that which is contrary to my will.

If I do not grow weary in declaring the Word of God, if I do not fear the people or seek my own life, if I do God's will, and keep His commandments; then I will be blessed forever, be made mighty in word, deed, faith, and works, and all things will be done according to my word, for my word will be one with God's will.

Although this remarkable covenant was made with Nephi, I include it to demonstrate the grand possibilities. We do not know of many others with whom such a covenant was made, but we do know that God is not a "respecter of persons" (Acts 10:34). If we live worthily and if Heavenly Father needs someone with such tremendous faith and power, then He may call upon you or me to act in His name in bringing forth His just cause.

> **12:1** And thus we can behold how false, and also the unsteadiness of the hearts of the children of men; yea, we can see that the Lord in his great infinite goodness doth bless and prosper those who put their trust in him.

If I put my trust in the Lord, then He will bless and prosper me.

> **12:22** And wo unto him to whom he shall say this, for it shall be unto him that will do iniquity, and he cannot be saved; therefore, for this cause, that men might be saved, hath repentance been declared.

If I do iniquity and do not repent, then I will be cut off from the presence of the Lord and will not be saved.

> **12:23** Therefore, blessed are they who will repent and hearken unto the voice of the Lord their God; for these are they that shall be saved.

If I repent and listen to and obey the voice of the Lord, then I will be saved.

13:6 Yea, heavy destruction awaiteth this people, and it surely cometh unto this people, and nothing can save this people save it be repentance and faith on the Lord Jesus Christ, who surely shall come into the world, and shall suffer many things and shall be slain for his people.

11 But if ye will repent and return unto the Lord your God I will turn away mine anger, saith the Lord; yea, thus saith the Lord, blessed are they who will repent and turn unto me, but wo unto him that repenteth not.

39 O ye people of the land, that ye would hear my words! And I pray that the anger of the Lord be turned away from you, and that ye would repent and be saved.

If I exercise faith in the Lord Jesus Christ, turn to Him, and repent of my sins, then the Lord will turn His anger away from me, bless me, and I will be saved.

14:2 And behold, he said unto them: Behold, I give unto you a sign; for five years more cometh, and behold, then cometh the Son of God to redeem all those who shall believe on his name.

8 And it shall come to pass that whosoever shall believe on the Son of God, the same shall have everlasting life.

13 And if ye believe on his name ye will repent of all your sins, that thereby ye may have a remission of them through his merits.

If I believe in Jesus Christ and repent of my sins, then my sins will be remitted. I will be saved and have everlasting life through Him.

14:18 Yea, and it bringeth to pass the condition of repentance, that whosoever repenteth the same is not hewn

> down and cast into the fire; but whosoever repenteth not is hewn down and cast into the fire; and there cometh upon them again a spiritual death, yea, a second death, for they are cut off again as to things pertaining to righteousness

If I repent, then I will not be hewn down and cast into the fire.

If I do not repent, then I will be hewn down and cast into the fire, suffer a spiritual death, and be cut off from righteousness.

> **14:19** Therefore repent ye, repent ye, lest by knowing these things and not doing them ye shall suffer yourselves to come under condemnation, and ye are brought down unto this second death.

If I know what I should do, but do not do it, then I will come under condemnation and suffer the second death.

> **14:29** And this to the intent that whosoever will believe might be saved, and that whosoever will not believe, a righteous judgment might come upon them; and also if they are condemned they bring upon themselves their own condemnation.

This verse speaks of the agency we have—to accept or reject the gospel.

If I will believe, then I will be saved.

If I will not believe, then a righteous judgment will come upon me, and I will bring upon myself my own condemnation.

14:30 And now remember, remember, my brethren, that whosoever perisheth, perisheth unto himself; and whosoever doeth iniquity, doeth it unto himself; for behold, ye are free; ye are permitted to act for yourselves; for behold, God hath given unto you a knowledge and he hath made you free.
31 He hath given unto you that ye might know good from evil, and he hath given unto you that ye might choose life or death; and ye can do good and be restored unto that which is good, or have that which is good restored unto you; or ye can do evil, and have that which is evil restored unto you.

God has given me my agency to make choices. He has given me knowledge of good and evil, and with that knowledge, I have the opportunity to choose life or death.

If I use my agency to choose good, then I will have good restored to me.

If I use my agency to choose evil, then I will have evil restored to me.

15:1 And now, my beloved brethren, behold, I declare unto you that except ye shall repent your houses shall be left unto you desolate.

If I do not repent, then my house, my eternal family, will be left desolate.

15:3 Yea, wo unto this people who are called the people of Nephi except they shall repent, when they shall see all these signs and wonders which shall be showed unto them; for behold, they have been a chosen people of the Lord; yea, the people of Nephi hath he loved, and also hath he chastened them; yea, in the days of their iniquities hath he chastened them because he loveth them.

If I do not repent, even after witnessing all the signs and wonders of my day, then woe will befall me.

If the Lord loves me, then He will chasten me.

15:7 And behold, ye do know of yourselves, for ye have witnessed it, that as many of them as are brought to the knowledge of the truth, and to know of the wicked and abominable traditions of their fathers, and are led to believe the holy scriptures, yea, the prophecies of the holy prophets, which are written, which leadeth them to faith on the Lord, and unto repentance, which faith and repentance bringeth a change of heart unto them—

8 Therefore, as many as have come to this, ye know of yourselves are firm and steadfast in the faith, and in the thing wherewith they have been made free.

If I want to experience a change of heart and remain firm and steadfast in the faith, then I must exercise faith unto repentance.

15:14 Therefore I say unto you, it shall be better for them than for you except ye repent.

If I do not repent of my sins after knowing all that I have known, then Judgment Day will be better for my enemies than for me.

15:17 And now behold, saith the Lord, concerning the people of the Nephites: If they will not repent, and observe to

> do my will, I will utterly destroy them, saith the Lord, because of their unbelief notwithstanding the many mighty works which I have done among them; and as surely as the Lord liveth shall these things be, saith the Lord.

If I, like the Nephites, rebel against the Lord, do not repent, and do not do His will, then I will be destroyed.

3 Nephi

3:15 Yea, he said unto them: As the Lord liveth, except ye repent of all your iniquities, and cry unto the Lord, ye will in no wise be delivered out of the hands of those Gadianton robbers.

If I do not repent of my iniquities and if I do not pray to the Lord, then I will not be delivered from my enemies.

8:1 And now it came to pass that according to our record, and we know our record to be true, for behold, it was a just man who did keep the record—for he truly did many miracles in the name of Jesus; and there was not any man who could do a miracle in the name of Jesus save he were cleansed every whit from his iniquity

If I am cleansed fully from my iniquity, then I will do miracles in the name of Jesus Christ.

9:2 Wo, wo, wo unto this people; wo unto the inhabitants of the whole earth except they shall repent; for the devil laugheth, and his angels rejoice, because of the slain of the fair sons and daughters of my people; and it is because of their iniquity and abominations that they are fallen!

If I do not repent of my iniquities and abominations, then woe to me, for I will fall.

9:13 O all ye that are spared because ye were more righteous than they, will ye not now return unto me, and repent of your sins, and be converted, that I may heal you?

If I return to the Lord, repent of my sins, and am converted, then I will be healed.

To what type of healing is the Lord referring? My first thought would be a spiritual healing, but why not a physical, an emotional, or even a social healing?

9:14 Yea, verily I say unto you, if ye will come unto me ye shall have eternal life. Behold, mine arm of mercy is extended towards you, and whosoever will come, him will I receive; and blessed are those who come unto me.

If I come to the Lord, then He will receive me and I will be blessed with eternal life.

9:17 And as many as have received me, to them have I given to become the sons of God; and even so will I to as many as shall believe on my name, for behold, by me redemption cometh, and in me is the law of Moses fulfilled.

If I believe in the Son of God and receive Him, then I will become a son of God.

> **9:20** And ye shall offer for a sacrifice unto me a broken heart and a contrite spirit. And whoso cometh unto me with a broken heart and a contrite spirit, him will I baptize with fire and with the Holy Ghost, even as the Lamanites, because of their faith in me at the time of their conversion, were baptized with fire and with the Holy Ghost, and they knew it not.

If I come to the Lord and offer to Him a sacrifice of a broken heart and a contrite spirit, then I will be baptized with fire and the Holy Ghost.

> **9:22** Therefore, whoso repenteth and cometh unto me as a little child, him will I receive, for of such is the kingdom of God. Behold, for such I have laid down my life, and have taken it up again; therefore repent, and come unto me ye ends of the earth, and be saved.

If I repent and come to Christ as a little child, then the Lord will receive me.

If I repent and come to Him, then I will be saved.

> **10:6** O ye house of Israel whom I have spared, how oft will I gather you as a hen gathereth her chickens under her wings, if ye will repent and return unto me with full purpose of heart.

If I repent and return to the Lord with my whole heart, completely intent on following Him, then He will gather me under His wings.

To me, "wings" reminds me of love, protection, comfort, and warmth.

11:23 Verily I say unto you, that whoso repenteth of his sins through your words, and desireth to be baptized in my name, on this wise shall ye baptize them—Behold, ye shall go down and stand in the water, and in my name shall ye baptize them.

If I repent of my sins when I hear the Word of the Lord and desire to be baptized in His name, then I will be received unto baptism.

11:33 And whoso believeth in me, and is baptized, the same shall be saved; and they are they who shall inherit the kingdom of God.

If I believe in Jesus Christ and am baptized, then I will be saved and inherit the kingdom of God.

11:34 And whoso believeth not in me, and is not baptized, shall be damned.

If I do not believe in Jesus Christ and am not baptized, then I will be damned.

11:35 Verily, verily, I say unto you, that this is my doctrine, and I bear record of it from the Father; and whoso believeth in me believeth in the Father also; and unto him will the Father bear record of me, for he will visit him with fire and with the Holy Ghost.

If I believe in Jesus Christ, then I will believe in the Father also, and He will reveal the Son to me, and will visit me with fire and the Holy Ghost.

11:36 And thus will the Father bear record of me, and the Holy Ghost will bear record unto him of the Father and me; for the Father, and I, and the Holy Ghost are one.

37 And again I say unto you, ye must repent, and become as a little child, and be baptized in my name, or ye can in nowise receive these things.

If I repent and become as a little child, and am baptized in the name of Jesus Christ, then the Father will reveal the Son to me. The Holy Ghost will reveal the Father and the Son. I will come to know the Father, the Son, and the Holy Ghost.

11:38 And again I say unto you, ye must repent, and be baptized in my name, and become as a little child, or ye can in nowise inherit the kingdom of God.

If I do not repent, am not baptized, and do not become as a little child, then I will not inherit the kingdom of God.

11:39 Verily, verily, I say unto you, that this is my doctrine, and whoso buildeth upon this buildeth upon my rock, and the gates of hell shall not prevail against them.

If I build upon the doctrine of Jesus Christ, then the gates of hell will not prevail against me.

11:40 And whoso shall declare more or less than this, and establish it for my doctrine, the same cometh of evil, and is not built upon my rock; but he buildeth upon a sandy foundation, and the gates of hell stand open to receive such when the floods come and the winds beat upon them.

If I declare more or less than what Jesus Christ or His servants teach, and establish it for His doctrine, then I am not built upon the rock of Christ, but am built upon a sandy foundation, and hell stands open, ready to receive me when the floods of temptation come and the winds of adversity beat upon me.

12:1 And it came to pass that when Jesus had spoken these words unto Nephi, and to those who had been called, (now the number of them who had been called, and received power and authority to baptize, was twelve) and behold, he stretched forth his hand unto the multitude, and cried unto them, saying: Blessed are ye if ye shall give heed unto the words of these twelve whom I have chosen from among you to minister unto you, and to be your servants; and unto them I have given power that they may baptize you with water; and after that ye are baptized with water, behold, I will baptize you with fire and with the Holy Ghost; therefore blessed are ye if ye shall believe in me and be baptized, after that ye have seen me and know that I am.

If I give heed to those whom Jesus has called to minister to me, to whom He has given the power to baptize, then I will be blessed.

If I am baptized, then the Lord will baptize me with fire and with the Holy Ghost.

12:2 And again, more blessed are they who shall believe in your words because that ye shall testify that ye have seen me, and that ye know that I am. Yea, blessed are they who shall believe in your words, and come down into the depths of humility and be baptized, for they shall be visited with fire and with the Holy Ghost, and shall receive a remission of their sins.

If I believe in the words of the servants of the Lord, humble myself, and am baptized, then I will be visited with fire and with the Holy Ghost, and will receive a remission of my sins.

12:3 Yea, blessed are the poor in spirit who come unto me, for theirs is the kingdom of heaven.

4 And again, blessed are all they that mourn, for they shall be comforted.

5 And blessed are the meek, for they shall inherit the earth.

6 And blessed are all they who do hunger and thirst after righteousness, for they shall be filled with the Holy Ghost.

7 And blessed are the merciful, for they shall obtain mercy.

8 And blessed are all the pure in heart, for they shall see God.

9 And blessed are all the peacemakers, for they shall be called the children of God.

10 And blessed are all they who are persecuted for my name's sake, for theirs is the kingdom of heaven.

11 And blessed are ye when men shall revile you and persecute, and shall say all manner of evil against you falsely, for my sake;

12 For ye shall have great joy and be exceedingly glad, for great shall be your reward in heaven; for so persecuted they the prophets who were before you.

Covenants from the Beatitudes:

If I am poor in spirit and come to Christ, then I will inherit the kingdom of heaven.

If I mourn, then I will be comforted.

If I am meek, then I will inherit the earth.

If I hunger and thirst after righteousness, then I will be filled with the Holy Ghost.

If I am merciful, then I will obtain mercy.

If I am pure in heart, then I will see God.

If I am a peacemaker, then I will be called a child of God.

If I am persecuted for the name of Christ, then I will inherit the kingdom of heaven.

If men revile me, persecute me, and say all manner of evil against me for the name of Christ, then I will have great joy, be exceedingly glad, and great will be my reward in heaven.

> **12:20** Therefore come unto me and be ye saved; for verily I say unto you, that except ye shall keep my commandments, which I have commanded you at this time, ye shall in no case enter into the kingdom of heaven.

If I come to Christ, then I will be saved.

If I do not keep the commandments that the Lord has given me, then I will in no case enter into the kingdom of heaven.

> **12:21** Ye have heard that it hath been said by them of old time, and it is also written before you, that thou shalt not kill, and whosoever shall kill shall be in danger of the judgment of God;

If I kill, then I will be in danger of the judgment of God.

12:22 But I say unto you, that whosoever is angry with his brother shall be in danger of his judgment. And whosoever shall say to his brother, Raca, shall be in danger of the council; and whosoever shall say, Thou fool, shall be in danger of hell fire.

If I am angry with my brother and use profane and unholy words against him, then I will be in danger of his judgment.

12:23 Therefore, if ye shall come unto me, or shall desire to come unto me, and rememberest that thy brother hath aught against thee—

24 Go thy way unto thy brother, and first be reconciled to thy brother, and then come unto me with full purpose of heart, and I will receive you.

If I desire to come to Christ but I know my brother has something against me, I must first go to my brother and be reconciled with him, then I can be reconciled with Christ.

If I come to Christ with my whole heart, completely intent on following Him, then He will receive me.

12:44 But behold I say unto you, love your enemies, bless them that curse you, do good to them that hate you, and pray for them who despitefully use you and persecute you;

45 That ye may be the children of your Father who is in heaven; for he maketh his sun to rise on the evil and on the good.

If I love my enemy, bless those who curse me, do good to those who hate me, and pray for those who spitefully use me and persecute me, then I will be a child of my Father in heaven.

> **13:1** Verily, verily, I say that I would that ye should do alms unto the poor; but take heed that ye do not your alms before men to be seen of them; otherwise ye have no reward of your Father who is in heaven.
>
> 2 Therefore, when ye shall do your alms do not sound a trumpet before you, as will hypocrites do in the synagogues and in the streets, that they may have glory of men. Verily I say unto you, they have their reward.
>
> 3 But when thou doest alms let not thy left hand know what thy right hand doeth;
>
> 4 That thine alms may be in secret; and thy Father who seeth in secret, himself shall reward thee openly.

If I do my alms before men, to be seen by them, then I will have no reward in heaven.

If I do my alms in secret, then Heavenly Father, who sees in secret, will reward me openly.

> **13:6** But thou, when thou prayest, enter into thy closet, and when thou hast shut thy door, pray to thy Father who is in secret; and thy Father, who seeth in secret, shall reward thee openly.

If I pray in secret, then Heavenly Father, who sees in secret, will reward me openly.

> **13:14** For, if ye forgive men their trespasses your heavenly Father will also forgive you;

15 But if ye forgive not men their trespasses neither will your Father forgive your trespasses.

If I forgive men their trespasses, then Heavenly Father will also forgive me.

If I do not forgive others, then Heavenly Father will not forgive me.

13:16 Moreover, when ye fast be not as the hypocrites, of a sad countenance, for they disfigure their faces that they may appear unto men to fast. Verily I say unto you, they have their reward.

17 But thou, when thou fastest, anoint thy head, and wash thy face;

18 That thou appear not unto men to fast, but unto thy Father, who is in secret; and thy Father, who seeth in secret, shall reward thee openly.

If I fast only to be seen by men, then I have my reward.

If I fast in secret, then Heavenly Father, who sees in secret, will reward me openly.

13:33 But seek ye first the kingdom of God and his righteousness, and all these things shall be added unto you.

If I first seek the kingdom of God and His righteousness, then all my other needs will be filled. (See verses 25–34.)

14:1 And now it came to pass that when Jesus had spoken these words he turned again to the multitude, and did open his mouth unto them again, saying: Verily, verily, I say unto you, Judge not, that ye be not judged.

2 For with what judgment ye judge, ye shall be judged; and with what measure ye mete, it shall be measured to you again.

If I judge, then I will be judged with that same judgment.

To whatever degree of good or evil I do to another, then I will receive the same in return. I believe that Heavenly Father will be just as generous to me as I am with others.

14:7 Ask, and it shall be given unto you; seek, and ye shall find; knock, and it shall be opened unto you.

8 For every one that asketh, receiveth; and he that seeketh, findeth; and to him that knocketh, it shall be opened.

If I ask, then it will be given me. If I seek, then I will find it. If I knock, then it will be opened to me.

14:19 Every tree that bringeth not forth good fruit is hewn down, and cast into the fire.

You may recall that the children of Israel were compared to an olive tree in the Allegory of the Olive Tree recorded in chapter 5 of Jacob. Often, throughout the Scriptures, the Lord compares us to a fruit tree and our works to the fruit.

If I do not bring forth good fruit, then I will be hewn down and cast into the fire.

14:21 Not every one that saith unto me, Lord, Lord, shall enter into the kingdom of heaven; but he that doeth the will of my Father who is in heaven.

If I do the will of my Father in heaven, then I will enter into the kingdom of heaven.

14:24 Therefore, whoso heareth these sayings of mine and
doeth them, I will liken him unto a wise man, who built his
house upon a rock—
25 And the rain descended, and the floods came, and the
winds blew, and beat upon that house; and it fell not, for it was
founded upon a rock.
26 And every one that heareth these sayings of mine and
doeth them not shall be likened unto a foolish man, who built
his house upon the sand—
27 And the rain descended, and the floods came, and the
winds blew, and beat upon that house; and it fell, and great was
the fall of it.

If I am wise and build my life upon the sure foundation of Jesus Christ by hearing His sayings and doing them, then when trials, temptations, and other adversities come, I will stand sure.

If I hear the sayings of Jesus Christ, but am foolish and do not do what He says to do, then when trials, temptations, and other adversities come, I will fall.

15:1 And now it came to pass that when Jesus had ended these sayings he cast his eyes round about on the multitude, and said unto them: Behold, ye have heard the things which I taught before I ascended to my Father; therefore, whoso remembereth these sayings of mine and doeth them, him will I raise up at the last day.

If I remember Christ's teachings and do what they require, then He will raise me up at the last day.

15:9 Behold, I am the law, and the light. Look unto me, and endure to the end, and ye shall live; for unto him that endureth to the end will I give eternal life.

If I look to Christ and endure to the end, then I will live and He will give me eternal life.

17:3 Therefore, go ye unto your homes, and ponder upon the things which I have said, and ask of the Father, in my name, that ye may understand, and prepare your minds for the morrow, and I come unto you again.

If I ponder the words of Christ and ask the Father in His name for greater understanding, then my mind will be prepared for further instruction.

18:7 And this shall ye do in remembrance of my body, which I have shown unto you. And it shall be a testimony unto the Father that ye do always remember me. And if ye do always remember me ye shall have my Spirit to be with you.

10 And when the disciples had done this, Jesus said unto them: Blessed are ye for this thing which ye have done, for this is fulfilling my commandments, and this doth witness unto the Father that ye are willing to do that which I have commanded you.

11 And this shall ye always do to those who repent and are baptized in my name; and ye shall do it in remembrance of my blood, which I have shed for you, that ye may witness unto the Father that ye do always remember me. And if ye do always remember me ye shall have my Spirit to be with you.

The Sacramental Covenants:

If I partake of the bread in remembrance of the body of Christ, as a testimony to the Father that I always remember Him, and that I am willing to take upon myself His name and do all that He commands me, then I will always have His Spirit to be with me.

If I drink of the wine in remembrance of the blood of Christ, witnessing to the Father that I always remember Him, then I will always have His Spirit to be with me.

> **18:12** And I give unto you a commandment that ye shall do these things. And if ye shall always do these things blessed are ye, for ye are built upon my rock.
> 13 But whoso among you shall do more or less than these are not built upon my rock, but are built upon a sandy foundation; and when the rain descends, and the floods come, and the winds blow, and beat upon them, they shall fall, and the gates of hell are ready open to receive them.
> 14 Therefore blessed are ye if ye shall keep my commandments, which the Father hath commanded me that I should give unto you.

If I always do what Heavenly Father has commanded me, then I will be blessed, and will be built upon Jesus Christ.

If I add to or subtract from the teachings of Jesus Christ, then I will fall.

> **18:15** Verily, verily, I say unto you, ye must watch and pray always, lest ye be tempted by the devil, and ye be led away captive by him.

If I always watch and pray, then I will not be tempted by the devil and will not be led away captive by him.

> **18:20** And whatsoever ye shall ask the Father in my name, which is right, believing that ye shall receive, behold it shall be given unto you.

If I ask the Father in the name of Jesus Christ, believing that I will receive, then it will be given unto me.

> **18:21** Pray in your families unto the Father, always in my name, that your wives and your children may be blessed.

If I pray within my family to the Father, in the name of Jesus Christ, then my wife and my children will be blessed.

> **18:25** And ye see that I have commanded that none of you should go away, but rather have commanded that ye should come unto me, that ye might feel and see; even so shall ye do unto the world; and whosoever breaketh this commandment suffereth himself to be led into temptation.

If I break the commandments, then I will be led into temptation.

> **18:29** For whoso eateth and drinketh my flesh and blood unworthily eateth and drinketh damnation to his soul; therefore if ye know that a man is unworthy to eat and drink of my flesh and blood ye shall forbid him.

If I eat and drink the Lord's flesh and blood unworthily, then I eat and drink damnation to my soul.

18:33 Therefore, keep these sayings which I have commanded you that ye come not under condemnation; for wo unto him whom the Father condemneth.

If I keep the commandments of the Lord, then I will not be condemned.

20:8 And he said unto them: He that eateth this bread eateth of my body to his soul; and he that drinketh of this wine drinketh of my blood to his soul; and his soul shall never hunger nor thirst, but shall be filled.

If I eat the bread, then the sacrifice of His body becomes a blessing to my soul.

If I drink the wine, then the shedding of His blood becomes a blessing to my soul.

If I eat the bread and drink the wine, then my soul will never hunger or thirst, but will be filled with the Holy Ghost.

20:23 Behold, I am he of whom Moses spake, saying: A prophet shall the Lord your God raise up unto you of your brethren, like unto me; him shall ye hear in all things whatsoever he shall say unto you. And it shall come to pass that every soul who will not hear that prophet shall be cut off from among the people.

If I do not hear the voice of Jesus Christ, Joseph Smith, or any of the prophets since, then I will be cut off from the covenant people.

21:11 Therefore it shall come to pass that whosoever will not believe in my words, who am Jesus Christ, which the Father shall cause him to bring forth unto the Gentiles, and shall give unto him power that he shall bring them forth unto the Gentiles, (it shall be done even as Moses said) they shall be cut off from among my people who are of the covenant.

If I do not believe in the words of Jesus Christ that will come forth to me, then I will be cut off from God's covenant people.

21:14 Yea, wo be unto the Gentiles except they repent; for it shall come to pass in that day, saith the Father, that I will cut off thy horses out of the midst of thee, and I will destroy thy chariots;

If I do not repent, then woe will befall me.

21:20 For it shall come to pass, saith the Father, that at that day whosoever will not repent and come unto my Beloved Son, them will I cut off from among my people, O house of Israel;

21 And I will execute vengeance and fury upon them, even as upon the heathen, such as they have not heard.

If I do not repent and come to Christ, then I will be cut off from the Lord's people, and God will execute vengeance and fury upon me.

21:22 But if they will repent and hearken unto my words, and harden not their hearts, I will establish my church among them, and they shall come in unto the covenant and be numbered among this the remnant of Jacob, unto whom I have given this land for their inheritance;

If men will repent, hearken unto Christ's words, and not harden their hearts, then He will establish His church among them. They will come into the covenant and be numbered among the remnant of Jacob.

23:5 And whosoever will hearken unto my words and repenteth and is baptized, the same shall be saved. Search the prophets, for many there be that testify of these things.

If I hearken to the words of Christ, repent, and am baptized, then I will be saved.

24:7 Even from the days of your fathers ye are gone away from mine ordinances, and have not kept them. Return unto me and I will return unto you, saith the Lord of Hosts. But ye say: Wherein shall we return?

If I return to the Lord, then the Lord will return to me.

24:10 Bring ye all the tithes into the storehouse, that there may be meat in my house; and prove me now herewith, saith the Lord of Hosts, if I will not open you the windows of heaven, and pour you out a blessing that there shall not be room enough to receive it.

11 And I will rebuke the devourer for your sakes, and he shall not destroy the fruits of your ground; neither shall your vine cast her fruit before the time in the fields, saith the Lord of Hosts.

12 And all nations shall call you blessed, for ye shall be a delightsome land, saith the Lord of Hosts.

If I pay my tithing, then the Lord will open the windows of heaven and pour out so many blessings upon me that I will not have enough room to receive them. He will rebuke the devourer for my sake. The fruit of my garden will not be destroyed, the vine will not bear its fruit before its time, and all nations will call me blessed.

24:16 Then they that feared the Lord spake often one to another, and the Lord hearkened and heard; and a book of remembrance was written before him for them that feared the Lord, and that thought upon his name.
17 And they shall be mine, saith the Lord of Hosts, in that day when I make up my jewels; and I will spare them as a man spareth his own son that serveth him.

If I revere the Lord and remember Him, then a book of remembrance will be written for me. I will be the Lord's in the day when He gathers His children.

25:1 For behold, the day cometh that shall burn as an oven; and all the proud, yea, and all that do wickedly, shall be stubble; and the day that cometh shall burn them up, saith the Lord of Hosts, that it shall leave them neither root nor branch.

If I am wicked and proud, then I will be burned up at the coming of the Lord, and be sealed to neither my ancestors nor my descendants.

25:2 But unto you that fear my name, shall the Son of Righteousness arise with healing in his wings; and ye shall go forth and grow up as calves in the stall.

If I revere the Lord, then I will be healed, protected, and saved through the atonement of Jesus Christ.

26:5 If they be good, to the resurrection of everlasting life; and if they be evil, to the resurrection of damnation; being on a parallel, the one on the one hand and the other on the other hand, according to the mercy, and the justice, and the holiness which is in Christ, who was before the world began.

If my works are good, then I will be resurrected to everlasting life.

If my works are evil, then I will be resurrected to damnation.

26:9 And when they shall have received this, which is expedient that they should have first, to try their faith, and if it shall so be that they shall believe these things then shall the greater things be made manifest unto them.

10 And if it so be that they will not believe these things, then shall the greater things be withheld from them, unto their condemnation.

If I believe the Scriptures that I have already received, then I will gain greater knowledge and revelation.

If I do not believe the Scriptures, then greater knowledge will be withheld, to my condemnation.

27:6 And whoso taketh upon him my name, and endureth to the end, the same shall be saved at the last day.

If I take upon myself the name of Christ and endure to the end, then I will be saved at the last day.

27:7 Therefore, whatsoever ye shall do, ye shall do it in my name; therefore ye shall call the church in my name; and ye shall call upon the Father in my name that he will bless the church for my sake.
9 Verily I say unto you, that ye are built upon my gospel; therefore ye shall call whatsoever things ye do call, in my name; therefore if ye call upon the Father, for the church, if it be in my name the Father will hear you;

Speaking to the church, Jesus commanded that we should do all things in His name.

If we pray to the Father in the name of Christ, then He will hear us and bless the church for Christ's sake.

27:10 And if it so be that the church is built upon my gospel then will the Father show forth his own works in it.
11 But if it be not built upon my gospel, and is built upon the works of men, or upon the works of the devil, verily I say unto you they have joy in their works for a season, and by and by the end cometh, and they are hewn down and cast into the fire, from whence there is no return.

If the church is built upon the gospel of Jesus Christ, then the Father will show forth His own works in it.

If the church is not built upon the gospel of Jesus Christ, then it will be hewn down and cast into the fire.

27:16 And it shall come to pass, that whoso repenteth and is baptized in my name shall be filled; and if he endureth to the end, behold, him will I hold guiltless before my Father at that day when I shall stand to judge the world.
17 And he that endureth not unto the end, the same is he that is also hewn down and cast into the fire, from whence they can no more return, because of the justice of the Father.

If I repent and am baptized, then I will be filled with the Holy Ghost.

If I endure to the end, then Christ will hold me guiltless before the Father at the Day of Judgment.

If I do not endure to the end, then I will be hewn down and cast into the fire, from which there is no return.

27:19 And no unclean thing can enter into his kingdom; therefore nothing entereth into his rest save it be those who have washed their garments in my blood, because of their faith, and the repentance of all their sins, and their faithfulness unto the end.

If I am unclean, then I cannot enter into the kingdom of God.

If through my faith I repent and am faithful to the end, then I will be clean and enter into the kingdom of God and into His rest.

27:20 Now this is the commandment: Repent, all ye ends of the earth, and come unto me and be baptized in my name, that ye may be sanctified by the reception of the Holy Ghost, that ye may stand spotless before me at the last day.

If I repent, come to Christ, and am baptized in His name, then I will be sanctified by the reception of the Holy Ghost and stand spotless before God at the last day.

> **27:21** Verily, verily, I say unto you, this is my gospel; and ye know the things that ye must do in my church; for the works which ye have seen me do that shall ye also do; for that which ye have seen me do even that shall ye do;
> 22 Therefore, if ye do these things blessed are ye, for ye shall be lifted up at the last day.

If I do the works Jesus did, then I will be blessed and lifted up at the last day.

> **27:28** And now I go unto the Father. And verily I say unto you, whatsoever things ye shall ask the Father in my name shall be given unto you.
> 29 Therefore, ask, and ye shall receive; knock, and it shall be opened unto you; for he that asketh, receiveth; and unto him that knocketh, it shall be opened.

We need to remember that in these verses, the Lord is speaking to the twelve whom He chose to minister to the people on the American continent. Many of us may not yet possess the same level of faith and understanding that these men had, so we need to remember Christ's teaching in 3 Nephi 18:20. It reads, "And whatsoever ye shall ask the Father in my name, *which is right* [emphasis mine], believing that ye shall receive, behold it shall be given unto you."

Whatsoever I shall ask the Father (which is right) shall be given to me.

If I ask, then I shall receive.

If I knock, then it shall be opened to me.

28:34 And wo be unto him that will not hearken unto the words of Jesus, and also to them whom he hath chosen and sent among them; for whoso receiveth not the words of Jesus and the words of those whom he hath sent receiveth not him; and therefore he will not receive them at the last day;

If I do not hearken to the words of Jesus, or to the words of those He has chosen and sent to me, then I have not received Jesus, and He will not receive me at the last day.

29:4 And when ye shall see these sayings coming forth among you, then ye need not any longer spurn at the doings of the Lord, for the sword of his justice is in his right hand; and behold, at that day, if ye shall spurn at his doings he will cause that it shall soon overtake you.

If I spurn the Lord's doings, then His justice will overtake me.

29:5 Wo unto him that spurneth at the doings of the Lord; yea, wo unto him that shall deny the Christ and his works!

If I deny Christ and His works, then I will bring a curse on myself.

29:6 Yea, wo unto him that shall deny the revelations of the Lord, and that shall say the Lord no longer worketh by revelation, or by prophecy, or by gifts, or by tongues, or by healings, or by the power of the Holy Ghost!

If I deny the revelations of the Lord, or say that the Lord no longer works by revelation, by prophecy, by gifts, by tongues, by healings, or by the power of the Holy Ghost, then woe will befall me.

29:7 Yea, and wo unto him that shall say at that day, to get gain, that there can be no miracle wrought by Jesus Christ; for he that doeth this shall become like unto the son of perdition, for whom there was no mercy, according to the word of Christ!

If I teach false doctrine to get gain, then woe will befall me. I will be like the son of perdition, for whom there was no mercy.

30:2 Turn, all ye Gentiles, from your wicked ways; and repent of your evil doings, of your lyings and deceivings, and of your whoredoms, and of your secret abominations, and your idolatries, and of your murders, and your priestcrafts, and your envyings, and your strifes, and from all your wickedness and abominations, and come unto me, and be baptized in my name, that ye may receive a remission of your sins, and be filled with the Holy Ghost, that ye may be numbered with my people who are of the house of Israel.

Speaking to the Gentiles, those who have not yet been baptized:

If you turn from your wicked ways, repent of your evil doings, lying, deceiving, whoredoms, secret abominations, idolatries, murders, priestcrafts, envying, strifes, wickedness, and abominations, and come to Christ to be baptized, receive a remission of your sins, and be filled with the Holy Ghost, then you will be numbered with Christ's people—the house of Israel.

4 Nephi

1:1 And it came to pass that the thirty and fourth year passed away, and also the thirty and fifth, and behold the disciples of Jesus had formed a church of Christ in all the lands round about. And as many as did come unto them, and did truly repent of their sins, were baptized in the name of Jesus; and they did also receive the Holy Ghost.

This verse shows the fulfillment of the covenant given by the Lord Jesus Christ to the unbelievers in 3 Nephi 30:2. Everyone who follows these steps that Jesus outlined for us will receive the same blessing.

After I truly repent of my sins and am baptized in the name of Jesus, then I will receive the gift of the Holy Ghost.

Mormon

5:24 Therefore, repent ye, and humble yourselves before him, lest he shall come out in justice against you—lest a remnant of the seed of Jacob shall go forth among you as a lion, and tear you in pieces, and there is none to deliver.

If I do not repent and humble myself before the Lord, then He will come out in justice against me.

7:7 And he hath brought to pass the redemption of the world, whereby he that is found guiltless before him at the judgment day hath it given unto him to dwell in the presence of God in his kingdom, to sing ceaseless praises with the choirs above, unto the Father, and unto the Son, and unto the Holy Ghost, which are one God, in a state of happiness which hath no end.

If I am found guiltless before God on Judgment Day, then I will dwell in the presence of God in His kingdom.

7:10 And ye will also know that ye are a remnant of the seed of Jacob; therefore ye are numbered among the people of the first covenant; and if it so be that ye believe in Christ, and are baptized, first with water, then with fire and with the Holy Ghost, following the example of our Savior, according to that which he hath commanded us, it shall be well with you in the day of judgment. Amen.

If I believe in Christ, am baptized with water, fire, and the Holy Ghost, and follow the example of my Savior in keeping the commandments of God, then it will be well with me in the Day of Judgment.

8:12 And whoso receiveth this record, and shall not condemn it because of the imperfections which are in it, the same shall know of greater things than these. Behold, I am Moroni; and were it possible, I would make all things known unto you.

If I receive *The Book of Mormon* and do not condemn it, then I will know of greater things.

8:14 And I am the same who hideth up this record unto the Lord; the plates thereof are of no worth, because of the commandment of the Lord. For he truly saith that no one shall have them to get gain; but the record thereof is of great worth; and whoso shall bring it to light, him will the Lord bless.

15 For none can have power to bring it to light save it be given him of God; for God wills that it shall be done with an eye single to his glory, or the welfare of the ancient and long dispersed covenant people of the Lord.

16 And blessed be he that shall bring this thing to light; for it shall be brought out of darkness unto light, according to the

> word of God; yea, it shall be brought out of the earth, and it shall shine forth out of darkness, and come unto the knowledge of the people; and it shall be done by the power of God.

Some may think that this series of verses would only pertain to Joseph Smith, the great prophet of the restoration, whose privilege it was to bring forth this record. However, I believe that these verses can also apply to anyone who, acting in the name of Christ, brings this record to light in the lives of individuals who have not yet had the opportunity to read and study it, or who have never heard of it.

If I, by the power of God, seeking only His glory and the welfare of His children, bring this record to light, then I will be blessed. Just as this record was brought forth with an eye to the glory of God, so we, when bringing it to light must do the same.

> **8:17** And if there be faults they be the faults of a man. But behold, we know no fault; nevertheless God knoweth all things; therefore, he that condemneth, let him be aware lest he shall be in danger of hell fire.

If I condemn this record, *The Book of Mormon*, then I will be in danger of hell fire.

> **8:19** For behold, the same that judgeth rashly shall be judged rashly again; for according to his works shall his wages be; therefore, he that smiteth shall be smitten again, of the Lord.

If I judge rashly, then I will be judged rashly. I will receive my rewards according to my works.

If I smite, then I will be smitten.

> **8:21** And he that shall breathe out wrath and strifes against the work of the Lord, and against the covenant people of the Lord who are the house of Israel, and shall say: We will destroy the work of the Lord, and the Lord will not remember his covenant which he hath made unto the house of Israel—the same is in danger to be hewn down and cast into the fire;

If I speak wrath and threaten strife against the work of the Lord and His covenant people, and threaten to destroy His work, then I will be in danger of being hewn down and cast into the fire.

> **9:6** O then ye unbelieving, turn ye unto the Lord; cry mightily unto the Father in the name of Jesus, that perhaps ye may be found spotless, pure, fair, and white, having been cleansed by the blood of the Lamb, at that great and last day.

If I will turn to the Lord and cry mightily to the Father in the name of Jesus, then I may be found spotless, pure, fair, and white, having been cleansed by the blood of the Lamb, Jesus Christ.

> **9:21** Behold, I say unto you that whoso believeth in Christ, doubting nothing, whatsoever he shall ask the Father in the name of Christ it shall be granted him; and this promise is unto all, even unto the ends of the earth.

If I believe in Christ and doubt nothing, then whatsoever I ask the Father in the name of Christ will be granted to me.

9:23 And he that believeth and is baptized shall be saved, but he that believeth not shall be damned;

If I believe, and am baptized, then I will be saved.
If I do not believe, then I will be damned.

9:24 And these signs shall follow them that believe—in my name shall they cast out devils; they shall speak with new tongues; they shall take up serpents; and if they drink any deadly thing it shall not hurt them; they shall lay hands on the sick and they shall recover;

If I believe, then I will cast out devils, speak with new tongues, and take up serpents, and if I drink any deadly thing, it will not hurt me. I will lay hands on the sick and they will recover.

9:25 And whosoever shall believe in my name, doubting nothing, unto him will I confirm all my words, even unto the ends of the earth.

If I believe in Jesus Christ, doubting nothing, then He will confirm all His words to me.

9:26 And now, behold, who can stand against the works of the Lord? Who can deny his sayings? Who will rise up against the almighty power of the Lord? Who will despise the works of the Lord? Who will despise the children of Christ? Behold, all

> ye who are despisers of the works of the Lord, for ye shall wonder and perish.

If I despise the works of the Lord, then I will wonder and perish.

> **9:29** See that ye are not baptized unworthily; see that ye partake not of the sacrament of Christ unworthily; but see that ye do all things in worthiness, and do it in the name of Jesus Christ, the Son of the living God; and if ye do this, and endure to the end, ye will in nowise be cast out.

If I am baptized or partake of the Sacrament unworthily, then I will be cast out.

If I do all things worthy of the name of Jesus Christ, whose name I have taken upon myself through baptism, and endure to the end, then I will not be cast out.

Ether

2:9 And now, we can behold the decrees of God
concerning this land, that it is a land of promise; and
whatsoever nation shall possess it shall serve God, or they shall
be swept off when the fulness of his wrath shall come upon
them. And the fulness of his wrath cometh upon them when
they are ripened in iniquity.
10 For behold, this is a land which is choice above all other
lands; wherefore he that doth possess it shall serve God or
shall be swept off; for it is the everlasting decree of God. And
it is not until the fulness of iniquity among the children of the
land, that they are swept off.

This is a warning first to the Jaredites, second to the Nephites, and third to us today. The Jaredites and Nephites did not heed this warning—will we?

Whatsoever nation will possess this land (the western hemisphere), if they do not serve the Lord, then they will be swept off.

> **2:12** Behold, this is a choice land, and whatsoever nation shall possess it shall be free from bondage, and from captivity, and from all other nations under heaven, if they will but serve the God of the land, who is Jesus Christ, who hath been manifested by the things which we have written.

If the people who live on this land (the western hemisphere) will serve Jesus Christ, then they will be free from bondage, from captivity, and from all other nations under heaven.

> **2:15** And the brother of Jared repented of the evil which he had done, and did call upon the name of the Lord for his brethren who were with him. And the Lord said unto him: I will forgive thee and thy brethren of their sins; but thou shalt not sin any more, for ye shall remember that my Spirit will not always strive with man; wherefore, if ye will sin until ye are fully ripe ye shall be cut off from the presence of the Lord. And these are my thoughts upon the land which I shall give you for your inheritance; for it shall be a land choice above all other lands.

In this verse, the Lord again compares our lives to fruit. When the fruit is fully ripe, it is time to pick it. In the Allegory of the Olive Tree in Jacob 5, we learn that we can produce either good or evil fruit. If we produce good fruit, then we will regain the presence of the Lord and enjoy eternal life. If we grow evil fruit, then, when ripe, it will yield spiritual death.

If I sin until I am fully ripe, then I will be cut off from the presence of the Lord.

3:14 Behold, I am he who was prepared from the foundation of the world to redeem my people. Behold, I am Jesus Christ. I am the Father and the Son. In me shall all mankind have life, and that eternally, even they who shall believe on my name; and they shall become my sons and my daughters.

If I believe in the name of Jesus Christ, then I will have eternal life, and become His son or daughter.

4:6 For the Lord said unto me: They shall not go forth unto the Gentiles until the day that they shall repent of their iniquity, and become clean before the Lord.
7 And in that day that they shall exercise faith in me, saith the Lord, even as the brother of Jared did, that they may become sanctified in me, then will I manifest unto them the things which the brother of Jared saw, even to the unfolding unto them all my revelations, saith Jesus Christ, the Son of God, the Father of the heavens and of the earth, and all things that in them are.

If I repent of my iniquity, come clean before the Lord, exercise faith in Him, and become sanctified in Him, then the Lord will manifest to me the things that the brother of Jared saw.

4:8 And he that will contend against the word of the Lord, let him be accursed; and he that shall deny these things, let him be accursed; for unto them will I show no greater things, saith Jesus Christ; for I am he who speaketh.

If I contend against the Word of the Lord, or if I deny the promises of the Lord made in the previous verses, then I will be accursed, and the Lord will show to me no greater things.

> **4:11** But he that believeth these things which I have spoken, him will I visit with the manifestations of my Spirit, and he shall know and bear record. For because of my Spirit he shall know that these things are true; for it persuadeth men to do good.

If I believe the words Moroni taught in Ether 4:5–10, then the Lord will visit me with the manifestations of His Spirit, and I will know and bear testimony of them.

> **4:12** And whatsoever thing persuadeth men to do good is of me; for good cometh of none save it be of me. I am the same that leadeth men to all good; he that will not believe my words will not believe me—that I am; and he that will not believe me will not believe the Father who sent me. For behold, I am the Father, I am the light, and the life, and the truth of the world.

If I do not believe in Christ's words, then I do not believe in Him and that He lives.

If I do not believe the Son, then neither do I believe the Father who sent Him.

> **4:13** Come unto me, O ye Gentiles, and I will show unto you the greater things, the knowledge which is hid up because of unbelief.
>
> 14 Come unto me, O ye house of Israel, and it shall be made manifest unto you how great things the Father hath laid

up for you, from the foundation of the world; and it hath not come unto you, because of unbelief.

If the Gentiles come to the Lord, then He will show them the knowledge that has been hidden because of unbelief.

If the house of Israel does not receive manifestations or revelations of the Lord, then it is because of unbelief.

4:15 Behold, when ye shall rend that veil of unbelief which doth cause you to remain in your awful state of wickedness, and hardness of heart, and blindness of mind, then shall the great and marvelous things which have been hid up from the foundation of the world from you—yea, when ye shall call upon the Father in my name, with a broken heart and a contrite spirit, then shall ye know that the Father hath remembered the covenant which he made unto your fathers, O house of Israel.

16 And then shall my revelations which I have caused to be written by my servant John be unfolded in the eyes of all the people. Remember, when ye see these things, ye shall know that the time is at hand that they shall be made manifest in very deed.

If I remove the veil of unbelief that has caused me to remain in my awful state of wickedness, by calling upon the Father in the name of Jesus Christ with a broken heart and a contrite spirit, then I will see the great and marvelous things that have been hidden from me. As this takes place, I will see that the Father has remembered the covenant that He made with the house of Israel. I will understand the

Lord's revelations written by His servant John, and I will know that the time is at hand that they will be made known.

> **4:18** Therefore, repent all ye ends of the earth, and come unto me, and believe in my gospel, and be baptized in my name; for he that believeth and is baptized shall be saved; but he that believeth not shall be damned; and signs shall follow them that believe in my name.

If I repent and come to Jesus Christ, believe in His gospel, and am baptized in His name, then I will be saved, and signs will follow me.

If I do not believe, then I will be damned.

> **4:19** And blessed is he that is found faithful unto my name at the last day, for he shall be lifted up to dwell in the kingdom prepared for him from the foundation of the world. And behold it is I that hath spoken it. Amen.

If I am found faithful to the name of Jesus Christ at the last day, then I will be lifted up to dwell in the kingdom prepared for me from the foundation of the world.

> **5:5** And if it so be that they repent and come unto the Father in the name of Jesus, they shall be received into the kingdom of God.

If I repent and come to the Father in the name of Jesus, then I will be received into the kingdom of God.

> **8:22** And whatsoever nation shall uphold such secret combinations, to get power and gain, until they shall spread

> over the nation, behold, they shall be destroyed; for the Lord will not suffer that the blood of his saints, which shall be shed by them, shall always cry unto him from the ground for vengeance upon them and yet he avenge them not.

If I uphold secret acts of wickedness to get power and gain, then I will be destroyed.

> **9:20** And thus the Lord did pour out his blessings upon this land, which was choice above all other lands; and he commanded that whoso should possess the land should possess it unto the Lord, or they should be destroyed when they were ripened in iniquity; for upon such, saith the Lord: I will pour out the fulness of my wrath.

In 1 Nephi 2:20 and Ether 2:7–12, we learn that this land, the American continent, was preserved by the Lord to be given to a righteous people with the understanding that all who possess it would serve the Lord. His covenant to those who inherit the land is a simple one. If we as a nation do not possess this land in accordance with the will of the Lord, then when we are ripened in iniquity, His wrath will come upon us and we will be destroyed.

> **12:6** And now, I, Moroni, would speak somewhat concerning these things; I would show unto the world that faith is things which are hoped for and not seen; wherefore, dispute not because ye see not, for ye receive no witness until after the trial of your faith.

If I do not dispute because I have not seen, then I will receive a witness after the trial of my faith.

12:9 Wherefore, ye may also have hope, and be partakers of the gift, if ye will but have faith.

If I will have faith, then I can have hope and partake of the heavenly gift—salvation.

12:12 For if there be no faith among the children of men God can do no miracle among them; wherefore, he showed not himself until after their faith.

If I have no faith, then I can do no miracles.

12:18 And neither at any time hath any wrought miracles until after their faith; wherefore they first believed in the Son of God.

If I believe in the Son of God and exercise faith, then I will perform miracles.

12:26 And when I had said this, the Lord spake unto me, saying: Fools mock, but they shall mourn; and my grace is sufficient for the meek, that they shall take no advantage of your weakness;

If I am foolish and mock the Word of God, then I will mourn.

If I am meek, then the grace of the Lord will be sufficient for me.

12:27 And if men come unto me I will show unto them their weakness. I give unto men weakness that they may be humble; and my grace is sufficient for all men that humble themselves before me; for if they humble themselves before me, and have faith in me, then will I make weak things become strong unto them.

If I come to the Lord, then He will show me my weaknesses.

If I humble myself before the Lord and have faith in Him, then He will make my weaknesses become strengths.

12:29 And I, Moroni, having heard these words, was comforted, and said: O Lord, thy righteous will be done, for I know that thou workest unto the children of men according to their faith;

If I have faith in the Lord, then He will work with me.

12:30 For the brother of Jared said unto the mountain
Zerin, Remove—and it was removed. And if he had not had
faith it would not have moved; wherefore thou workest after
men have faith.
31 For thus didst thou manifest thyself unto thy disciples;
for after they had faith, and did speak in thy name, thou didst
show thyself unto them in great power.

If I exercise my faith, and speak in the name of the Lord, then He will manifest Himself to me in great power.

12:32 And I also remember that thou hast said that thou hast prepared a house for man, yea, even among the mansions of thy Father, in which man might have a more excellent hope; wherefore man must hope, or he cannot receive an inheritance in the place which thou hast prepared.

34 And now I know that this love which thou hast had for the children of men is charity; wherefore, except men shall have charity they cannot inherit that place which thou hast prepared in the mansions of thy Father.

If I have hope in God's promise that there is a house prepared for me in His mansions, and if I have charity for His children, then I will inherit that place God prepared for me.

12:41 And now, I would commend you to seek this Jesus of whom the prophets and apostles have written, that the grace of God the Father, and also the Lord Jesus Christ, and the Holy Ghost, which beareth record of them, may be and abide in you forever. Amen.

If I seek Jesus, of whom the prophets and apostles have written, then the grace of God the Father, the Lord Jesus Christ, and the Holy Ghost will be and abide in me forever

Moroni

2:2 And he called them by name, saying: Ye shall call on the Father in my name, in mighty prayer; and after ye have done this ye shall have power that to him upon whom ye shall lay your hands, ye shall give the Holy Ghost; and in my name shall ye give it, for thus do mine apostles.

If I call upon the Father in the name of Jesus Christ, then I will have power to bestow the Holy Ghost upon whomever I lay my hands.

4:3 O God, the Eternal Father, we ask thee in the name of thy Son, Jesus Christ, to bless and sanctify this bread to the souls of all those who partake of it; that they may eat in remembrance of the body of thy Son, and witness unto thee, O God, the Eternal Father, that they are willing to take upon them the name of thy Son, and always remember him, and keep his commandments which he hath given them, that they may always have his Spirit to be with them. Amen.

5:2 O God, the Eternal Father, we ask thee, in the name of thy Son, Jesus Christ, to bless and sanctify this wine to the souls of all those who drink of it, that they may do it in remembrance of the blood of thy Son, which was shed for them; that they may witness unto thee, O God, the Eternal Father, that they do always remember him, that they may have his Spirit to be with them. Amen.

If I partake of the Sacrament in remembrance of the body and blood of Jesus Christ, and witness to the Father that I am willing and do take the name of Jesus Christ, always remember Him, and keep His commandments, then I will always have His spirit with me.

6:8 But as oft as they repented and sought forgiveness, with real intent, they were forgiven.

If I repent and seek forgiveness with real intent, then I will be forgiven.

7:18 And now, my brethren, seeing that ye know the light by which ye may judge, which light is the light of Christ, see that ye do not judge wrongfully; for with that same judgment which ye judge ye shall also be judged.

If I judge wrongfully, then I will be judged by that same measure.

7:19 Wherefore, I beseech of you, brethren, that ye should search diligently in the light of Christ that ye may know good from evil; and if ye will lay hold upon every good thing, and condemn it not, ye certainly will be a child of Christ.

If I will search diligently in the light of Christ, that I may learn good from evil and lay hold of every good thing, and if I do not condemn it, then I will certainly be a child of Christ.

> **7:26** And after that he came men also were saved by faith in his name; and by faith, they become the sons of God. And as surely as Christ liveth he spake these words unto our fathers, saying: Whatsoever thing ye shall ask the Father in my name, which is good, in faith believing that ye shall receive, behold, it shall be done unto you.

If I exercise faith in Jesus Christ, then I will become a child of God and be saved.

If I ask Heavenly Father for good things in the name of Jesus Christ, with faith, believing that I will receive, then it will be given to me.

> **7:30** For behold, they are subject unto him, to minister according to the word of his command, showing themselves unto them of strong faith and a firm mind in every form of godliness.

If I have strong faith and am firm in mind in every form of godliness, then angels will minister to me according to the command of God.

> **7:33** And Christ hath said: If ye will have faith in me ye shall have power to do whatsoever thing is expedient in me.

If I will have faith in Christ, then I shall have power to do whatsoever thing is expedient in Him.

7:34 And he hath said: Repent all ye ends of the earth, and come unto me, and be baptized in my name, and have faith in me, that ye may be saved.

If I repent, come to Christ, am baptized in His name, and have faith in Him, then I will be saved.

7:38 For no man can be saved, according to the words of Christ, save they shall have faith in his name; wherefore, if these things have ceased, then has faith ceased also; and awful is the state of man, for they are as though there had been no redemption made.

If I do not have faith in Jesus Christ, then I cannot be saved.

If faith ceases, then miracles cease.

7:43 And again, behold I say unto you that he cannot have faith and hope, save he shall be meek, and lowly of heart.

44 If so, his faith and hope is vain, for none is acceptable before God, save the meek and lowly in heart; and if a man be meek and lowly in heart, and confesses by the power of the Holy Ghost that Jesus is the Christ, he must needs have charity; for if he have not charity he is nothing; wherefore he must needs have charity.

If I am meek, humble, and confess by the Holy Ghost that Jesus is the Christ, then I will have faith, hope, and charity. I will be acceptable to God!

If I do not have charity, then I am nothing.

7:47 But charity is the pure love of Christ, and it endureth forever; and whoso is found possessed of it at the last day, it shall be well with him.

If I am found possessing charity at the last day, then it will be well for me.

7:48 Wherefore, my beloved brethren, pray unto the Father with all the energy of heart, that ye may be filled with this love, which he hath bestowed upon all who are true followers of his Son, Jesus Christ; that ye may become the sons of God; that when he shall appear we shall be like him, for we shall see him as he is; that we may have this hope; that we may be purified even as he is pure. Amen.

If I pray to Heavenly Father with all energy of heart, then I will be filled with His love, and I will become a son of God, a true follower of Jesus Christ. I will see Him when He appears, and I will be pure even as He is pure.

8:10 Behold I say unto you that this thing shall ye teach—repentance and baptism unto those who are accountable and capable of committing sin; yea, teach parents that they must repent and be baptized, and humble themselves as their little children, and they shall all be saved with their little children.

If I repent, am baptized, and humble myself as my little children, then I will be saved with my little children.

9:6 And now, my beloved son, notwithstanding their hardness, let us labor diligently; for if we should cease to labor, we should be brought under condemnation; for we have a labor to perform whilst in this tabernacle of clay, that we may conquer the enemy of all righteousness, and rest our souls in the kingdom of God.

If I cease to labor, then I will be brought under condemnation.

If I labor while in the body, then I will conquer the enemy of righteousness, and my soul will rest in the kingdom of God.

9:22 But behold, my son, I recommend thee unto God, and I trust in Christ that thou wilt be saved; and I pray unto God that he will spare thy life, to witness the return of his people unto him, or their utter destruction; for I know that they must perish except they repent and return unto him.

If I do not repent and return to God, then I must perish.

10:3 Behold, I would exhort you that when ye shall read these things, if it be wisdom in God that ye should read them, that ye would remember how merciful the Lord hath been unto the children of men, from the creation of Adam even down until the time that ye shall receive these things, and ponder it in your hearts.

4 And when ye shall receive these things, I would exhort you that ye would ask God, the Eternal Father, in the name of Christ, if these things are not true; and if ye shall ask with a sincere heart, with real intent, having faith in Christ, he will manifest the truth of it unto you, by the power of the Holy Ghost.

5 And by the power of the Holy Ghost ye may know the truth of all things.

This promise can be applied to anything of which we want to know the truth, not simply *The Book of Mormon*.

If I will remember how merciful the Lord has been to His children, if I will ask God in the name of Christ whether this book is true, and if I ask with a sincere heart, a commitment to change, and faith in Christ; then He will manifest the truth of it to me by the power of the Holy Ghost. By the power of the Holy Ghost, I may know the truth of all things.

> **10:20** Wherefore, there must be faith; and if there must be faith there must also be hope; and if there must be hope there must also be charity.
>
> 21 And except ye have charity ye can in nowise be saved in the kingdom of God; neither can ye be saved in the kingdom of God if ye have not faith; neither can ye if ye have no hope.

If I have faith, then I must have hope; if I have hope, then I must have charity; and if I have charity, then I will be saved in the kingdom of God.

If I do not have faith or hope or charity, then I cannot be saved in the kingdom of God.

> **10:22** And if ye have no hope ye must needs be in despair; and despair cometh because of iniquity.

If I have no hope, then I must be in despair.

If I am in despair, then I am in the depths of iniquity.

> **10:23** And Christ truly said unto our fathers: If ye have faith ye can do all things which are expedient unto me.

If I have faith, then I can do all things that are expedient in Christ.

> **10:32** Yea, come unto Christ, and be perfected in him, and deny yourselves of all ungodliness; and if ye shall deny yourselves of all ungodliness, and love God with all your might, mind and strength, then is his grace sufficient for you, that by his grace ye may be perfect in Christ; and if by the grace of God ye are perfect in Christ, ye can in nowise deny the power of God.

If I come to Christ and am perfected in Him, deny all ungodliness, and love God with all my might, mind and strength, then His grace will be sufficient for me. By His grace I will be perfected in Him. Then there is no way I can deny the power of God.

> **10:33** And again, if ye by the grace of God are perfect in Christ, and deny not his power, then are ye sanctified in Christ by the grace of God, through the shedding of the blood of Christ, which is in the covenant of the Father unto the remission of your sins, that ye become holy, without spot.

If by the grace of God I am perfect in Christ, and I do not deny His power, then I will be sanctified in Him by the grace of God through the shedding of the blood of Christ.

This is the covenant of the Father to the remission of my sins, that I might become holy and blameless, without spot.

Appendix

The topics below are not all that could be listed. These are listed to help you do your own research. The Lord does not teach us all things in one short verse, but over many lessons, and much time. The Scriptures need to be searched in order to obtain a greater understanding of His expectations of us.

Who will succumb to their enemies? 31, 69, 98, 166, 173
Who will be led into temptation? 31, 87, 178, 185, 188
How can I find liberty and freedom? 41, 96, 159, 170, 171, 210
How can I be happy and have joy? 31, 32, 42, 45, 46, 48, 71, 86, 87, 88, 90, 91, 92, 93, 95, 105, 115, 118, 133, 136, 138, 144, 151, 154, 159, 162, 179, 180, 203
How can I witness signs, miracles and wonders? 51, 52, 53, 54, 55, 170, 171, 173, 207, 214, 216
How will the Lord work with me? 28, 30, 33, 34, 35, 36, 39, 43, 45, 47, 50, 55, 217
How can I become pure and delightsome? 58, 59, 60, 162, 191, 206
How can I speak with the tongue of angels? 60, 61, 62, 63
How can I become rich? 68
How can I be comforted and consoled? 68, 69, 106, 108, 137, 175, 179, 217
How can I loose myself from hell? 43, 44, 53, 69, 70, 127, 128, 133, 149, 177
How can I learn the commandments? 27, 28, 33, 34, 35, 36, 81, 82, 133, 191, 220, 221
How can I be filled with love? 83, 87, 88, 90, 91, 152, 223
How can I learn the mysteries of God? 26, 29, 83, 127, 128, 136, 137
How can I become a Saint? 47, 87, 96
How can I prepare for baptism? 60, 61, 62, 73, 106, 107, 123, 176, 223
How can I abound in the grace of God? 112, 216, 218, 226
How can I bring forth good works? 97, 120, 123, 124, 136, 137

Index

Bibliography

The Book of Mormon, Another Testament of Jesus Christ. Salt Lake City, Utah, U.S.A.: The Church of Jesus Christ of Latter-day Saints, 1981.

The Holy Bible. Salt Lake City, Utah, U.S.A: Corporation of the President of the Church of Jesus Christ of Latter-day Saints, 1979.

Acknowledgments

I extend my love and appreciation to my wife and children, who have shown their love, support, and patience for me during the time it has taken to prepare this work for publication.

I thank my parents for their encouragement.

I have been very blessed to find a willing publisher in American Book Publishing. My editor, Pav Cherny, has been wonderful; I pass on to him my heartfelt gratitude.

Finally, I thank L. Edward Brown for his inspired counsel that ultimately made it possible for this work to be published.

About The Author

Floyd W. Gowans is a retired B-52 navigator and bombardier. During the 20 years of service to his country, he lived in many different parts of the United States and visited many parts of the world. Floyd served in a range of positions in numerous Branches, Wards and Stakes. Currently, he is serving a part-time service mission as a host in the Conference Center of the Church of Jesus Christ of Latter-day Saints and as High Priest Group Leader in his ward. Tybrin Corporation at Hill Air Force Base, Utah, employs him as a B-52 subject matter expert in mission planning systems.

Floyd is a native of Salt Lake City, Utah. He received a bachelor's degree in business from Brigham Young University and a master's degree from National University.

Floyd is married to the former Karen Neal of Salt Lake City and has five children: Mrs. Shannon E. Wilkinson, Mrs. Becky M. Costanzo, Jacob W., Rosalee, and Adam N. Gowans.